Marijuana

DRUGS The Straight Facts

Alcohol

Cocaine

Hallucinogens

Heroin

Marijuana

Nicotine

■ DRUGS
The Straight Facts

Marijuana

Randi Mehling

Consulting Editor
David J. Triggle
University Professor
School of Pharmacy and Pharmaceutical Sciences
State University of New York at Buffalo

CHELSEA HOUSE
P U B L I S H E R S
A Haights Cross Communications ▼ Company
P h i l a d e l p h i a

CHELSEA HOUSE PUBLISHERS
VP, NEW PRODUCT DEVELOPMENT Sally Cheney
DIRECTOR OF PRODUCTION Kim Shinners
CREATIVE MANAGER Takeshi Takahashi
MANUFACTURING MANAGER Diann Grasse

Staff for MARIJUANA
ASSOCIATE EDITOR Bill Conn
PRODUCTION EDITOR Jamie Winkler
PICTURE RESEARCHER Sarah Bloom
SERIES & COVER DESIGNER Terry Mallon
LAYOUT 21st Century Publishing and Communications, Inc.

A Haights Cross Communications ⚓ Company

http://www.chelseahouse.com

3 5 7 9 8 6 4 2

Library of Congress Cataloging-in-Publication Data

Mehling, Randi.
    Marijuana / Randi Mehling.
        p. cm.—(Drugs, the straight facts)
Includes index.
    ISBN 0-7910-7263-0
    1. Marijuana—Juvenile literature. I. Title. II. Series.
HV5822.M3 M39 2002
613.8'35—dc21

                                    2002153569

Table of Contents

The Use and Abuse of Drugs

The issues associated with drug use and abuse in contemporary society are vexing subjects, fraught with political agendas and ideals that often obscure essential information that teens need to know to have intelligent discussions about how to best deal with the problems associated with drug use and abuse. *Drugs: The Straight Facts* aims to provide this essential information through straightforward explanations of how an individual drug or group of drugs works in both therapeutic and non-therapeutic conditions; with historical information about the use and abuse of specific drugs; with discussion of drug policies in the United States; and with an ample list of further reading.

From the start, the series uses the word *"drug"* to describe psychoactive substances that are used for medicinal or non-medicinal purposes. Included in this broad category are substances that are legal or illegal. It is worth noting that humans have used many of these substances for hundreds, if not thousands of years. For example, traces of marijuana and cocaine have been found in Egyptian mummies; the use of peyote and Amanita fungi has long been a component of religious ceremonies worldwide; and alcohol production and consumption have been an integral part of many human cultures' social and religious ceremonies. One can speculate about why early human societies chose to use such drugs. Perhaps, anything that could provide relief from the harshness of life—anything that could make the poor conditions and fatigue associated with hard work easier to bear—was considered a welcome tonic. Life was likely to be, according to the seventeenth century English philosopher Thomas Hobbes, *"poor, nasty, brutish and short."* One can also speculate about modern human societies' continued use and abuse of drugs. Whatever the reasons, the consequences of sustained drug use are not insignificant—addiction, overdose, incarceration, and drug wars—and must be dealt with by an informed citizenry.

The problem that faces our society today is how to break

the connection between our demand for drugs and the willingness of largely outside countries to supply this highly profitable trade. This is the same problem we have faced since narcotics and cocaine were outlawed by the Harrison Narcotic Act of 1914, and we have yet to defeat it despite current expenditures of approximately $20 billion per year on "the war on drugs." The first step in meeting any challenge is always an intelligent and informed citizenry. The purpose of this series is to educate our readers so that they can make informed decisions about issues related to drugs and drug abuse.

SUGGESTED ADDITIONAL READING

David T. Courtwright, *Forces of Habit. Drugs and the making of the modern world.* Cambridge, Mass.: Harvard University Press, 2001. David Courtwright is Professor of History at the University of North Florida.

Richard Davenport-Hines, *The Pursuit of Oblivion. A global history of narcotics.* New York: Norton, 2002. The author is a professional historian and a member of the Royal Historical Society.

Aldous Huxley, *Brave New World.* New York: Harper & Row, 1932. Huxley's book, written in 1932, paints a picture of a cloned society devoted to the pursuit only of happiness.

David J. Triggle
University Professor
School of Pharmacy and Pharmaceutical Sciences
State University of New York at Buffalo

1

The History of Marijuana

Marijuana is the flowering part of the Indian hemp plant *Cannabis sativa*, a weed-like species that grows wild and is also cultivated in many tropical and temperate parts of the world. *Cannabis* means "hemp" in Latin and is derived from the Greek word *kannabis*. Marijuana probably comes from the Mexican Spanish *marijuana/marihuana* (Mary's leaf or plant) or from Maria and Juan (Mary and John). Among its many names, marijuana is commonly known as weed, ganja, mary jane, and pot.

For thousands of years, cannabis has enjoyed historical significance as a recreational drug, a useful fiber, an oil, an edible seed, and a medicine. It has been used to aid religious practices, alter mood (psychoactive effect), stimulate creativity, treat disease, relieve anxiety and boredom, enhance sensory experience and pleasure, rebel against authority, and go along with peer influence. That is a lot of work for one plant to do. This probably explains why cannabis has always been an important cultivated crop and is currently a cornerstone of controversial debate in all sectors of U.S. and international society.

Despite society's focus on the marijuana "high," cannabis historically has provided many meaningful industrial and medicinal values that are not attributed to its psychoactive effects. Researchers discovered that cannabis crops farmed as far back as 12,000 years ago yielded hemp, a distinct variety of the cannabis plant associated with little or no psychoactivity. The first evidence of the medicinal use of cannabis can be traced to a Chinese health publication from

Marijuana, or *Cannabis sativa*, is a weed-like plant that grows in temperate and tropical climates. Although best known for its psychoactive properties and use as a recreational drug, marijuana has also been used historically for industrial and medicinal purposes not related to its mind altering abilities.

5,000 years ago, which listed cannabis as an herbal remedy. Cannabis probably originated in central Asia.

HISTORY OF HEMP IN AMERICA

Let's take a quick look at hemp and marijuana through American history, beginning with the colonists fresh from their trip from England.

The first American crop of Indian hemp was planted by English colonists in 1611 near Jamestown, Virginia. Cultivation of this plant for its fibrous content was mandated (ordered) by the colonists' mother country, England, which relied on the hemp plant for sails, ropes, linens, and paper. The American climate was considered ideal for growing hemp, and the English looked forward to an abundant yield. When Sir Walter Raleigh suggested to King James I that the land might be better suited for tobacco, which was just being introduced to Europe, King James I "firmly corrected" the future tobacco baron and ordered the colonists to produce hemp.

After the American Revolution, American settlers continued to grow hemp of excellent quality in the land now known as Kentucky. Hemp fiber continued to be a cash crop, the source of rope that rigged many of the world's sailing ships, and the rugged fabric that covered settlers' wagons as they made their way westward. Canvas, another hemp product, was widely used for sails in the shipping industry. A remarkably durable cloth, it is one of the few that seawater does not rot or mildew. (The word *canvas* is rooted in "cannabis.")

For centuries of American history, use of the cannabis plant as an intoxicant was rare. In fact, Kentucky pioneers cultivated tons of hemp without a single reference to its intoxicating properties. People probably didn't know of the use of cannabis as an intoxicant. Entries from George Washington's diary in 1765 show that he personally planted and harvested cannabis for both fiber and medicinal purposes.

By the early nineteenth century, the medicinal use of cannabis spread from Asia and the Middle East to Europe, and finally to the Americas by the mid 1800s. A Western physician named W.B. O'Shaughnessey who was working in Calcutta, India, observed the use of cannabis there. After performing tests on animals, the doctor assured himself that cannabis was safe. He developed a solution of cannabis in alcohol, known as a tincture. When placed in the mouth, this tincture proved an effective analgesic (pain reliever). The doctor was also impressed with its muscle relaxant and anticonvulsant (seizure preventive) qualities and brought his "tincture of marijuana" to the United States after publishing his study results in 1839.

Touting it as a nerve tonic, doctors began to prescribe tincture of marijuana for a variety of conditions. However, pharmacies posted a warning that large doses of this medicinal remedy were dangerous and considered narcotic (addictive). In addition, physicians found that cannabis stimulated the appetite. By 1887, dentists found hemp to be an excellent topical anesthetic for performing dental procedures on their patients. Cannabis was also found to be a powerful disinfectant.

CAN HEMP SAVE THE ENVIRONMENT?

Proponents of hemp cultivation for uses unrelated to its psychoactive effects often site the following environmental benefits of hemp over traditional materials:

- Hemp can be used as a substitute for cotton in clothing and linens. It is naturally resistant to most pests, eliminating the need for toxic pesticides. Cotton production uses 50 percent of all the world's pesticides.

- Hemp can be cultivated for wood and paper products every 100 days, whereas trees take years to grow back.

- Hemp, like trees, is an abundant source of cellulose, a basic component of plastic. However, 1 acre of hemp produces nearly as much cellulose as 4 acres of trees.

- Hemp contains the highest concentration of essential amino and fatty acids found in any food, and its protein content is second only to soy.

- There are over 25,000 economically feasible yet environmentally friendly uses for hemp, including diesel fuel, food and beauty products, insulation, textiles, paper, and paints.

A team of narcotics agents in Kentucky searches fields for a small crop of marijuana plants spotted from a helicopter. Despite attempts to enforce the law, some growers manage to evade authorities and sell their marijuana harvest illegally.

In the early part of the twentieth century, marijuana and hashish (concentrated resin from the hemp plant) became popular with artists and musicians, who felt that marijuana enhanced their creativity. Moreover, all sorts of excessive behavior, including violence and mental illness, became associated with marijuana. In 1936, a movie called *Tell Your Children* was financed by a small church group who wanted to deliver a strong cautionary message to parents about the "evils" of marijuana in a mock documentary format. Soon after the film was shot, it was re-edited and released as *Reefer Madness*. Today, many of the "deviant" behaviors portrayed in this movie are known to be greatly exaggerated. In its time, however, *Reefer Madness* was viewed by many as proof of marijuana's "menace to society."

As a result of these and other concerns, the Marihuana Tax Act was passed in 1937 with the intention of making recreational marijuana too expensive to obtain legally. Although not specifically aimed at the medical or hemp industry, this act (along with other legal restrictions) created the conditions that led to the removal of cannabis as a prescribed drug by 1941 and to the end of the once-prosperous hemp industry by the 1950s. Despite this attempt at restriction, marijuana use spread to other subgroups, and in the 1960s it became a prominent symbol of the youth movement on college campuses. Since then, marijuana has steadily become more popular, and today it is the most widely used of all illegal drugs.

Within the last 30 years, medical research has discovered new and potentially beneficial therapeutic effects of marijuana and THC (tetrahydrocannabinol, the primary active ingredient in marijuana). For example, it has been found that marijuana can reduce internal eye pressure in persons suffering from glaucoma. Similarly, it alleviates the nausea and vomiting that are often caused by chemotherapeutic drugs used to treat cancer patients. Because of its appetite-stimulating effects, marijuana has also been shown to help people suffering from cancer and AIDS to maintain their weight. And, marijuana may be able to reduce the pain and convulsions associated with multiple sclerosis and epilepsy in some patients.

2

The Properties and Effects of Marijuana

AN INTRODUCTION TO *CANNABIS SATIVA*

The chemical compounds primarily responsible for the psychoactive and medicinal properties of the hemp plant are concentrated in an aromatic, tar-like resin in the flowering tops of the Indian hemp plant (*Cannabis sativa*). This resin tends to be most potent in the female plants, especially when they are cultivated before the seeds form. (They are also known as *sinsemilla*, a Spanish word meaning "without seed.") It is said that the hemp plant produces the resin as protection from heat in order to preserve moisture during reproduction. The plants highest in resin therefore tend to grow in hot regions such as Mexico, the Middle East, and India.

It is the flowers, buds, or leaves of the hemp plant that are known as marijuana. The resin itself can be collected and pressed into cakes or lumps called hashish. In addition, the resin can be extracted into a thick, oily liquid known as hashish oil. Any of these preparations can be eaten or smoked.

The three most prevalent varieties of the Indian hemp plant are *Cannabis sativa* (*C. sativa*), the most common of the three varieties, which is tall, loosely branched, and grows as high as 20 feet; *Cannabis indica*, which is three or four feet in height, pyramidal in shape, and densely branched; and *Cannabis ruderalis*, which grows to a height of about two feet with few or no branches. There is disagreement over whether these three cannabis types are different species or whether *C. sativa* is the main species of Indian hemp, with the other plants

The resin of the flowering tops of the Indian hemp plant contain the chemical compounds responsible for marijuana's psychoactive and medicinal properties. This resin can be collected and pressed into blocks, known as hashish.

being just two of the many varieties of that species. Many recent scientific reports refer to the *C. sativa* plant; therefore, we will use "cannabis," "hemp plant," and "marijuana" interchangeably with *C. sativa*.

There are differences among these plants in the leaves, stems, and, most important, the resin. The resin content determines the the effective strength of a hemp preparation; yet the resin amount can vary greatly from plant to plant. Hashish, a more concentrated form of resin, is about eight times stronger than marijuana. Cannabis bred specifically for industrial use with little or no

15

THC

This is the chemical structure of THC, or tetrahydrocannabinol — the only psychoactive compound present in large amounts in marijuana resin. THC content varies with the genetic strain and maturity of the plant.

psychoactive properties is usually known as hemp and is used in a multitude of products such as clothing and food.

CANNABINOIDS AND THC

The psychoactive and medicinal chemical compounds found in the resin of the marijuana plant are known as cannabinoids. The cannabis plant contains more than 460 known compounds; over 60 of these have a cannabinoid structure. The only cannabinoid that is highly psychoactive and present in large amounts in the resin of the cannabis plant is tetrahydrocannabinol, or THC. The other two major cannabinoids are the cannabidiols and the cannabinols. It appears that the cannabis plant first produces the mildly active cannabidiols, which are converted to the more psychoactive THCs and then broken down to relatively inactive cannabinols as the plant matures. Therefore, the THC content can vary, depending on the genetic strain of the plant and its degree of maturity.

When protected from exposure to air and light, marijuana may retain its THC content for many months. Other THCs exist that are roughly as potent as THC, but they are found in much smaller quantities and in only a few varieties of cannabis.

Cannabis may be smoked like a cigarette (a "joint"), or in a water pipe (a "bong") or a regular pipe (a "bowl"). Smokers typically inhale deeply and hold their breath to maximize the amount of THC absorption by the lungs. Marijuana can also be eaten and is sometimes prepared in brownies or other baked goods.

POTENCY OF THC

Some studies indicate that the THC content of cannabis rose dramatically from the 1960s to the 1990s. The increase is assumed to be a result of different growing and breeding methods. As a result, many researchers and policymakers believe that it is possible that today's marijuana users are experiencing a much more potent, and therefore more dangerous, drug than previous users. Although these researchers report an increase in the THC levels from the 1960s to the 1990s, they also report that the average THC level in cannabis has been relatively stable in recent years.

Other researchers disagree with the theory of increased THC levels. They argue that the original studies showing this increase were faulty because they were based on samples of marijuana with lower-than-average THC content—not representative of the marijuana available years ago. Thus, today's THC potency is overstated. These researchers assert that the average potency of THC in today's marijuana remains relatively unchanged; yet they acknowledge that more potent marijuana at the "high end of the spectrum" is more widely available today than previously.

Research also suggests that marijuana with a high THC content is not necessarily more dangerous to the user; however, very potent levels can increase adverse physical and psychological effects in those who are not used to marijuana's effects. Various research sources indicate that there are no documented cases of fatal overdose from smoking or eating marijuana, regardless of THC content. In studying the amount of THC that would kill rats (the lethal dose), scientists were unable to establish a comparable lethal dose in primates such as monkeys, which are genetically similar to humans.

Aside from this controversy, recent research shows that the THC content of marijuana ranges from 0.5 to 5.0 percent, and the THC in hashish ranges from 2 to 20 percent. Hashish oil may contain between 15 to 50 percent THC, and sinsemilla varieties may have a THC content of up to 20 percent. Many studies indicate that marijuana of less than 0.5 percent potency has basically no psychoactivity. However, every individual's reaction to the psychoactive effects of THC is different. Some reports indicate that what marijuana users may term "bad trips" have been recorded with marijuana that ranges from quite low (0.7 percent THC content) to quite high (7.5 percent THC content).

IN A CLASS BY ITSELF

A common definition of the word "drug" is any substance that in small amounts produces significant changes in the body or mind. Psychoactive drugs such as marijuana affect the mind, thoughts, perceptions, and especially moods. Although marijuana is considered by many to be a mild psychedelic (producing abnormal or distorted psychic effects), its effects are different from hallucinogens (drugs that distort perceptions of reality). Marijuana is neither a stimulant nor a depressant, but has characteristics of both. Unlike hallucinogens and other drugs, marijuana can be used frequently or even continually while one goes about daily activities. This creates strong possibilities for abuse.

Marijuana is also distinctive because it is soluble in oil, but not in water. As a result, THC accumulates in fat cells. Although many drugs enter the body's fat cells in a similar fashion to marijuana, most drugs exit the body quickly. Since THC exits the fat cells slowly, traces of THC are detectable in the body for days or weeks after inhaling or ingesting it. Several studies indicate that active THC can leave fat cells and re-enter the bloodstream, creating a subtle high for up to 24 hours. Other researchers cite evidence that the psychoactive effects of THC wear off within two to four hours after use, even in frequent users. Nevertheless, there is little evidence to suggest that there are harmful short-term or long-term effects on the fat cells where THC lingers.

A WORD ABOUT DOSE

Before discussing the short-term and long-term physical effects of marijuana, we need to say a word about dose. Any substance, whether a drug or even water, can benefit or harm a person, depending on its quantity and potency. High doses of a substance can produce very different effects from those of low doses. Water is necessary for human life, but drink extreme

TOLERANCE AND DEPENDENCE

The concept of tolerance is important in understanding the properties and effects of marijuana. Tolerance can be defined as the need for increasing doses of a drug over time to maintain the same effect achieved at previous lower doses. Receptors in the brain develop a tolerance to THC. Since the body becomes tolerant to the effects of marijuana, heavy users often feel a decreasing effect from the drug and thus may need to smoke ever-increasing quantities to achieve the earlier "high." Because of this, we can see why tolerance is an important characteristic of dependence on marijuana.

amounts of it in a short period of time, and the electrolyte and other critical balances in the body can be disrupted with very negative consequences. Many medicines are beneficial at low doses, but deadly at high doses.

TWO SIDES OF EVIDENCE

Much has been written about the negative effects of marijuana on the human body. Before proceeding, it is important to note that an extensive review of the literature reveals much uncertainty about this. Marijuana is the most widely used illicit (illegal) drug among adolescents—among the entire population, in fact—and opinions are polarized on each side of an often raging debate.

The *New Encyclopaedia Brittanica* says "There have been extensive studies on cannabis, but there is little definitive information to support any firm conclusions regarding its use." Dr. Andrew Weil, Harvard-trained physician and a noted alternative health specialist, says, "Arguments about marijuana tend to be more political than factual. And because pharmacologists and medical doctors are just as caught up in the politics of marijuana as other people, it's difficult to get neutral information about the drug. Much marijuana research sets out to prove preconceived ideas, and much of it is not worth reading." Dr. Eric A. Voth, medical director of Chemical Dependency Services and a prominent voice of scientists who show evidence of marijuana's harmful effects, contends, "Under the false and dangerous claims that smoking marijuana is a harmless recreational activity . . . the drug culture seeks to use bogus information to gain public acceptance for the legalization of marijuana."

Whom do we believe? Each side of the marijuana debate presents evidence to support its theory while disputing the other's. For example, much of the literature that suggests there are harmful effects from marijuana is based on studies that used massive doses of THC on test animals—far beyond the doses used by even heavy marijuana users. Such study results need to be carefully weighed to see if they are relevant to humans. In addition, study results must be able to be duplicated in order to be regarded as scientifically valid. Many of the studies showing adverse health effects of THC were unable to reproduce their results in subsequent studies.

The same questions need to be asked of the many studies that show little or no ill effects from marijuana: Have these researchers been fair and balanced in their approaches? Remember to think critically and explore all sides before forming an opinion.

THE PHYSICAL AND PSYCHOLOGICAL EFFECTS OF MARIJUANA

Euphoria. Anxiety. Clumsiness. Forgetfulness. Hunger. Pain relief. Creative thinking. Panic attacks. Racing heart. Mouth dryness. Bloodshot eyes. Paranoia. Relaxation. Tiredness. Sensory awareness. Poor coordination. Uncontrollable laughter.

The short-term effects of marijuana are extremely variable, unpredictable, and temporary. Just as each person looks different, each person's biochemistry is different. Two people can respond differently to the same dose of the same drug, and an individual can even feel different effects from the same dose of marijuana from one experience to the next. One person may feel euphoric (having an exaggerated feeling of well-being) after smoking marijuana and feel very positive about the experience, and another may feel similar sensations, yet feel disoriented. Most of the phenomena of marijuana are directly dose-related and individual, so it is difficult to categorize its physical and psychological effects.

There are probably as many descriptions of the physical and psychological effects of marijuana as there are people who use it. Some of the more common physical effects from smoking or eating marijuana are rapid heart beat, dry mouth, bloodshot eyes, increased hunger, slower coordination, difficulty in following a train of thought, and short-term memory loss. Many studies support THC's medicinal capacity to ease pain and nausea, decrease ocular pressure, and control convulsions. Typical psychological effects are anxiety, panic attacks, feelings of paranoia, confusion, relaxation and stress

A s Harry and Rod walked toward their high school, Harry seemed out of sorts. "Want to smoke a bowl before class?" he asked. Rod smiled and nodded. The boys ducked into an alley next to a dry cleaner about a block from school. Harry pulled a wooden pipe out of his back pocket, and Rod shook his head, "You are takin' chances, man! Anyone could of seen that in your pocket there!" Harry smirked and pulled a lighter out of his backpack. He packed the bowl with pot and handed the pipe to Rod. After a few hits, Rod exhaled loudly and leaned against the brick-faced building.

"So, what's up? Why the gloom and doom face?"

Harry grimaced and shrugged his shoulders nonchalantly. "They're gonna hold me back if my grades don't get better — so what? That counselor says I've gotta stop smoking . . . and he knows . . . so what?" Harry laughed and faked a punch to Rod's gut. "Let's get outta here. Old Ms. Frannie'll have our skin for being late again to homeroom!"

Harry and Rod may not know that they could be smoking their future away. Marijuana has been shown to affect short-term memory and learning functions of the brain. Also, a person who is high has difficulty learning and retaining important information while in school. If Harry and Rod get arrested for possessing or using pot, they may not be eligible for student loans, small business loans, farm subsidies, or government grants. This could affect their future ability to attend college or start up a business.

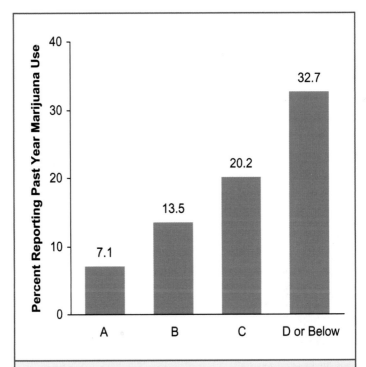

The short-term effects of marijuana use include an impairment of short-term memory and learning. A survey of 12- to 17-year-old students found a correlation between past-year marijuana use and lower grade averages. However, this survey did not take into consideration possible pre-existing behavioral problems that may have also influenced grade averages.

reduction, and increased awareness for music, joy, and sensory experiences.

Consequences of the short-term effects of marijuana can greatly influence a teen's future life. Short-term acute effects describe a condition that is temporary and short-lived; long-term chronic effects are cumulative and can last a lifetime. Many studies document the acute and chronic health consequences of smoking marijuana. For instance, there are consistent reports that marijuana temporarily impairs short-term memory and learning. This is confirmed by users of marijuana outside the laboratory, in which many people report that a marijuana high affects their ability to concentrate on one thing and to sustain a train of thought. These studies suggest that in real-world structured settings, such as the classroom, marijuana is very likely to have similar effects. One cannot predict with assurance the long-term effect of going to school and getting high, but it is reasonable to assume that a student who consistently attends school while high will likely not be able to retain the valuable information needed for future endeavors, including college or professional enterprise.

It is also worth noting that there are no assurances that any given quantity of marijuana is "pure." Marijuana sprayed with herbicides or pesticides can be toxic and is thus capable of causing serious long-term health effects. Paraquat, for instance, is a very poisonous herbicide used to kill unwanted plants. In 1975, American drug enforcement authorities encouraged Mexican officials to spray paraquat on illegal marijuana fields. Despite this, the sprayed marijuana was still harvested and smuggled into the United States for sale. This spraying program has since been halted.

DEFINING THE EFFECTS OF MARIJUANA

To define the effects of marijuana, pharmacologists give drugs to animals and people while they are in controlled laboratory settings. These scientists study the effects of drugs in humans by trying to isolate drug reactions and then predict why some people experience particular physical and psychological responses to marijuana and some do not. They also seek to determine what reaction might surface in response to a particular situation.

Dose

Especially in the laboratory, dose is a crucial variable in predicting human responses to marijuana. However, it is important to be aware that controlled laboratory experiments often do not correlate with actual real-world experiences. Why? In addition to dose, two other factors influence both the short-term and the long-term effects of marijuana: a person's "set" of expectations when using marijuana and the "setting" in which marijuana is used.

Set

Set is a person's expectation for the type of effect he or she will experience after using marijuana. This expectation is created by a person's total past experience–what he or she has ever heard, read, seen, or thought about encounters with marijuana. Sometimes teenagers (just like adults) do not really know what their deep-down feelings are about using marijuana. One person could feel eager to "fit in" with friends and could think smoking marijuana is cool, but really be scared of what might happen— of losing control, for example. Based on these conscious and unconscious expectations, in a given situation a person's underlying feelings can determine the effect from a marijuana experience as much as the particular dosage of the drug.

Setting

Setting is a person's physical, social, and cultural environment. In ancient India, marijuana was eaten for religious purposes, and people used it for its medicinal and psychoactive properties in socially accepted ways. In England and America during the nineteenth century, physicians gave a tincture of marijuana to sick people as a remedy. Most patients did not report getting high on it, probably because they did not expect this outcome. This is another example of set. Through set and setting, we can see that the effects of drugs are specific to specific people, places, and times. This awareness demonstrates part of the reason why it can be difficult to draw certain conclusions from scientific predictions of marijuana's effects outside a controlled laboratory.

People who smoke or eat marijuana for the first time often

report that they feel no effect, even if they use high doses of potent marijuana. This is another way to look at a person's set and setting; it seems to take practice to know how to "be high." Also, each particular individual needs to understand and define what the expectations are for being high. In other words, people have to learn to associate changes of consciousness with the physical effects of the drug.

ROUTES OF EXPOSURE

How does marijuana affect the body? To answer this question, we must ascertain how THC gains access to the body (the route of exposure). Routes of exposure may be as important as dose when considering implications to human health, since they strongly influence the body's response to marijuana.

The major routes through which marijuana may enter the body are inhalation and ingestion. The greatest effect with the most rapid response is produced when THC is inhaled. This is because smoking bypasses the digestive process and travels directly to the central nervous system (the brain) by means of the bloodstream. Because of this fast-acting and direct route to the nervous system, studies suggest that high doses of inhaled drugs can be more harmful and more addicting over time. In addition, a marijuana user controls the amount of drug entering the body by controlling the portion of the marijuana cigarette smoked. In this way, the cigarette can be considered a drug delivery device.

The body's systems respond more slowly after marijuana is eaten. People who ingest marijuana, which may be cooked and incorporated into a meal, experience a slower onset of effects because the drug has to first go through the digestive process before it reaches the bloodstream and is carried to the central nervous system. The stomach absorbs marijuana unevenly after it is eaten owing to the fat-soluble properties of THC. Regardless of whether THC is inhaled or ingested, heat is required to convert marijuana to its psychoactive properties because of its fat solubility. Thus, simply eating a raw cannabis plant is not likely to produce a high.

THE MARIJUANA HIGH

Whether marijuana is inhaled or ingested, when THC enters the bloodstream it is delivered to the brain and the central nervous system. When the amount of THC in the brain exceeds a certain dose, a "high" is experienced, usually within 15 to 30 minutes.

In addition to reaching the brain, THC is delivered to all other parts of the body. This distribution eventually reduces the amount of THC in the blood; in turn, this reduces the amount of THC in the brain. Within two to four hours, THC levels in the brain typically fall below what is necessary for psychoactivity, and the user "comes down" from the high. Eventually, THC is eliminated from the body in sweat, feces, and urine.

EFFECTS OF MARIJUANA ON
THE CENTRAL NERVOUS SYSTEM

Drugs do not contain highs; drugs trigger these highs. The potential for feeling high exists naturally within the human nervous system, and we have countless options for getting high without taking drugs. Small children love to spin wildly in circles. Many people go sky diving, fall in love, paint, meditate—the list is endless.

Marijuana triggers a high via the central nervous system (CNS). The CNS controls the functions of the brain and the spinal cord. There are billions of nerve cells called neurons within the CNS that are linked by an intricate web of synapses (the gaps between neurons). Perhaps you seek to move a finger to relieve the itch of a bug bite. To do this, the neurons responsible for moving your finger need to communicate with each other. The message "move my finger" is transmitted simultaneously along the neuronal system of synapses by means of neurotransmitters, which are chemicals released by the neurons to help neurons communicate with each other. Neurons are also known as messenger cells, and neurotransmitters as chemical messengers.

Neurotransmitters can be envisioned as keys that unlock specific sites on neurons called receptors. A neurotransmitter opens the receptor's lock, and it is through this key-and-lock system that messages are conveyed throughout the CNS. Most receptors are specifically tuned to accept only one type of neurotransmitter key. Hormones can also act as keys that unlock certain receptor sites. Some neurons have thousands of receptors that are specific to particular neurotransmitters.

THC IN THE BRAIN AND BODY

A cannabinoid is a type of chemical compound concentrated in the resin of the cannabis plant. THC is the only cannabinoid that is highly psychoactive and present in large amounts in cannabis. Until recently, there has been little information on precisely how THC acts on the brain, which cells are affected by THC, or even what general areas of the brain are most affected by it. All this changed in the 1980s and 1990s with the discovery of specific cannabinoid receptors—Cannabinoid receptor 1 (CB1) and Cannabinoid receptor 2 (CB2).

CB1 is found predominantly in the brain and is associated with many of the effects from THC. CB2 is found in the spleen and other organs and is associated with the immune system; its role is still not fully understood. The discovery of these receptors, as well as their locations in the body, has allowed scientists to learn more about how marijuana affects the human brain and body.

CB1 and CB2 can be found throughout the human body; hence, there are a variety of ways that cannabinoids can physically and psychologically affect the body's systems. As an example, the presence of CB1 receptors in the eye may explain how marijuana eases glaucoma and relieves intraocular pressure. Other research indicates that THC can block receptors in the brain and body to produce dizziness, dry mouth, and altered depth perception—all common effects of marijuana use. There appears to be an

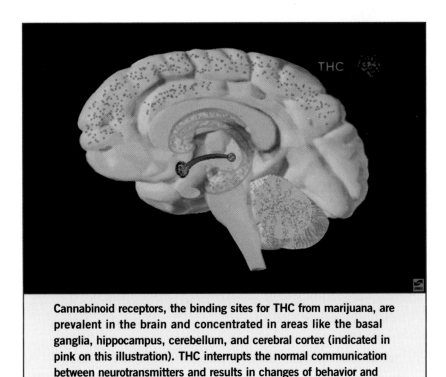

Cannabinoid receptors, the binding sites for THC from marijuana, are prevalent in the brain and concentrated in areas like the basal ganglia, hippocampus, cerebellum, and cerebral cortex (indicated in pink on this illustration). THC interrupts the normal communication between neurotransmitters and results in changes of behavior and physical effects controlled by these areas of the brain.

endless array of research studies that can match THC's effects with an appropriate action at a particular cannabinoid receptor site. Herein lies the ability of science to advance medicinal breakthroughs: Numerous ongoing research investigations are underway to explore site-specific medications that would specifically alleviate pain, for example, without causing dizziness or euphoria. This process is termed "selective uptake."

AGONISTS AND ANTAGONISTS

Remember, the primary job of the neurotransmitter is to fit or "lock" into its own particular receptor, and then to initiate specific physiological responses within the body. However, many drugs, such as THC, are able to bind or attach themselves to a specific receptor, thus mimicking or blocking the normal function of the neurotransmitter destined for that receptor. Some drugs are agonists that activate or "turn on" receptors, and some are antagonists that block receptor function. It is not even that straightforward: many receptors in the brain are linked so that activation of one may block the function of another. These linkages are created by a variety of cellular messengers whose function is to relay information from inside neurons or from one neuron to another.

Thus, proper functioning of the nervous system relies on balancing the results of these receptor activations, regardless if the receptor is activated by a drug mimicking or blocking a neurotransmitter or by the specific neurotransmitter itself. This balance is found between the "excitatory" (stimulant) actions of neurotransmitters and the "inhibitory" (depressant) actions of neurotransmitters. As an example, let us look at a drug that acts like an antagonist that blocks the inhibitory action of a neuro-transmitter. This blockade could upset the balance of normal neuronal function by allowing excitatory activity to become the more dominant neuronal action. In a myriad of ways, these types of neuronal imbalances can be translated to the physical and psychological effects that are seen after using drugs such as marijuana. In this manner, we can see that the actions of agonists and antagonists can be quite complex.

ENDOGENOUS (INTERNALLY PRODUCED) CANNABINOIDS

There are many examples of naturally-occurring plants that contain drugs that interact with neuronal receptors, including THC, nicotine, morphine, LSD, and cocaine. The effects that result from the use of these drugs, both desirable and undesir-able, are determined through their actions at specific receptors. Scientists have long wondered why nature would create receptors in the human body that could be activated by chemicals in plants. Clearly, these receptors did not evolve simply to recognize THC from ingesting or smoking the cannabis plant, nicotine from

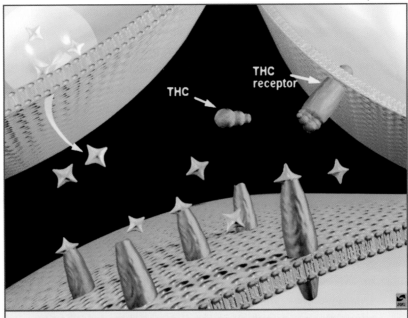

When marijuana is ingested or inhaled, THC binds to cannabinoid receptors throughout the brain and body, where it mimics the actions of internally produced neurotransmitters, such as the endocannabinoid known as anandamide. Anandamide is named after the Sanskrit word *ananda*, which means "bliss."

smoking a cigarette, or morphine from eating the resin from the poppy plant. As we have discussed, receptors exist to interact with specific neurotransmitters. For example, acetylcholine locks into the acetylcholine receptor. However, nicotine also acts at this receptor, as does THC. Why?

Once scientists established the general validity of the receptor/neurotransmitter process, they explored this question more deeply, asking: If drugs such as morphine and THC act at receptors in the brain, then are there internally produced (endogenous) neurotransmitters in our brains designed for those same receptors? If so, then are morphine, THC, and other drugs simply surrogates for these endogenous neurotransmitters?

The answer is yes. In the 1970s, scientists found that the brain produces morphine-like narcotics called endorphins (*endo*genous *morphin*es) that activate the opiate receptors in the brain. Morphine also attaches to opiate receptors; therefore, it is actually mimicking the effects of these human-produced endorphins that create the euphoria and reduction in pain often experienced by a morphine user.

Similar reasoning led scientists in 1993 to the discovery of the endogenous cannabinoid called anandamide that binds to cannabinoid receptors. Because THC also binds to these receptors, it therefore mimics the actions of anandamide. Anandamide produces THC-like effects, and in fact was named from the Sanskrit word *ananda*, meaning "bliss." Although other endogenous cannabinoids have been found in the body, the precise role of all the endocannabinoids (*endo*genous *cannabinoids*) is not well established at this time, although very recent evidence suggests that they may be involved in memory processes.

Many scientists believe that anandamide, endorphins, and other endogenous drugs create the "highs" we experience, such as from running or being in love. Some people may produce more of these endogenous chemicals than others, or may have more sensitive receptors. It may be possible that those who do not produce many of these receptors are the ones who find marijuana, opiates, or other drugs particularly pleasant and may come to rely upon them for this externally produced "high." This is especially evident in those individuals with depression, schizophrenia, and other mental disorders. It is known that people with these types of mental illnesses actually have imbalances in their central neurotransmitter systems. These imbalances can be corrected, at least in part, by antidepressants and other medications that assist in balancing actions at critical receptor sites.

CANNABINOID RECEPTORS AND BRAIN FUNCTIONS

CB1 receptors are widely prevalent in the brain and are particularly concentrated in areas known as the basal ganglia, hippocampus, cerebellum, and cerebral cortex. By binding or blocking actions of the cannabinoid receptors, THC interrupts normal neuronal communications and so creates the effects that are associated with marijuana usage. Studies now show that the behavioral and physical effects associated with THC and marijuana strongly correlate with the amounts of cannabinoid receptors in these areas of the brain.

For example, scientific and anecdotal research shows that marijuana can impair coordination and other motor skills in humans. (As with other effects, these are dose-dependent.) The highest number of CB1 receptors can be found in the basal ganglia, a part of the brain that regulates body movements. CB1 receptors are also abundant in the cerebellum, which is responsible for coordination and movement; the hippocampus, which is involved in the learning process, memory, and response to stress; and the cerebral cortex, where higher cognitive functions such as problem-solving are integrated. Short-term memory loss has been associated with temporary lesions that form in the hippocampal region of the brain.

3

The Health Effects of Marijuana

Acute effects of THC can be severe but are usually short-lived and temporary. Current literature documents THC's "temporary" effect on health, suggesting that once the use of marijuana ceases, a rapid recovery from the drug's effects typically occurs.

However, equating "temporary" with "benign" (harmless) would be misleading because some of marijuana's so-called temporary effects can last a lifetime. For example, studies have shown that driving while high can increase the possibility of a motor vehicle accident. In this case, the consequences of marijuana's short-term effects (impaired attention, motor skills, and reaction times) might quickly transform "temporary" to "permanent."

Chronic effects are frequent, habitual, and long-term. Investigators are also very interested in the chronic health effects of marijuana and THC and their influence on the lives of teenagers. The scientific literature discusses health effects of marijuana on bodily systems.

THE IMMUNE SYSTEM

How do you define health? Many would say health is more than just the absence of disease; rather, a healthy person tends to be happy and vital, feeling physically and mentally centered and balanced. The immune system is the body's foundation for feeling healthy. It plays a critical role in protecting the body from illness. It even has a backup system so that if one part of our immunity is compromised, another mechanism is ready to participate in the body's protection and wellness.

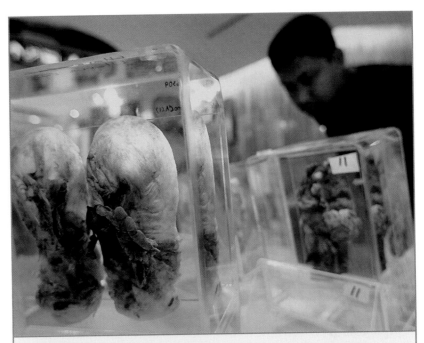

This man examines the preserved lungs of a lung cancer victim who smoked cigarettes. Although no definitive evidence connects long-term marijuana smoking with cancer, precancerous cells have been found in the lungs and respiratory tracts of heavy marijuana smokers.

Much research has focused on marijuana's effects on the immune system. Some research has shown that one type of immune system cell called the macrophage (scavenger cell) is particularly sensitive to THC exposure. Macrophages clear the body of viruses, bacteria, and particles that are inhaled or ingested. These studies found the presence of cannabinoid receptors on macrophages, suggesting that THC can disrupt normal immune system functions and may eventually inhibit the body's natural immune response.

Other researchers dispute evidence of the harmful effects of THC on the immune system. They take issue with the design of these immune studies, pointing out that the animals studied were given extremely high doses of THC, sometimes more than 1,000 times the amount actually required for a human to get high. (After exposing the animals to these high doses, an increase in infections was reported.) Because of these high dosages, these researchers say the outcomes of such studies have little relevance to humans.

Researchers also have difficulty correlating a diminished immune function with THC exposure. Some found that the short-term "immunosuppressive effects" of THC were not well established. Others note that because heavy marijuana smokers can tend to have erratic lifestyles, they may increase their chances of infection or illness simply by lowering their immune function through poor sleep and nutrition.

THE RESPIRATORY SYSTEM

The scientific community seems to agree that damage to the lungs is the main physiological risk from marijuana because smoking is the preferred method of getting high from marijuana. This may be because the effects from marijuana are almost instantaneous when inhaled. In other words, THC bypasses the digestive system and goes directly from the lungs into the bloodstream. Indeed, after an extensive scientific investigation, experts at the Institute of Medicine found that the health effects from marijuana are shown to be temporary in most of the body's major systems, with the exception of the lungs. (This comprehensive report was commissioned by the Office of National Drug Control Policy, which reports directly to the President of the United States.)

Studies indicate that both the acute and chronic effects from smoking marijuana often mirror the short-term and long-term effects associated with smoking tobacco. Smoke is made up of both solid and gas particles. The inhalation of hot gases combined with volatile tars (and other particulates) can be very harmful to the lungs, throat, and bronchial tubes. Short-term health effects from smoking marijuana can include an increase in phlegm (mucus), chest congestion, wheezing, coughing fits, and respiratory infections. Chronic effects of marijuana smoking are associated with bronchitis and pneumonia.

In addition, precancerous cells have been found in the lungs and respiratory tracts of some heavy long-term marijuana smokers. Although no definitive evidence correlates long-term marijuana smoking and cancer, some of the evidence has led researchers to speculate that there may be similar connections between smoking marijuana and smoking-related illnesses after years of even moderate marijuana smoking. Since the prevention of cancer is often at the heart of public and scientific concern, most of the scientific literature is advising more long-term studies on humans to establish whether habitual marijuana smoking does or does not cause cancer.

In studying marijuana smoke and its health effects, some researchers directly compared heavy marijuana smokers with tobacco smokers. (Heavy marijuana smokers in this study were defined as those who had been smoking an average of three to four marijuana cigarettes per day for about 15 years.) These studies found that one marijuana cigarette deposits four times as much tar in the lungs as one tobacco cigarette. The studies also showed that the tar in marijuana smoke contains 50 percent more of certain carcinogenic (cancer-causing) ingredients than tobacco smoke contains. Researchers hypothesize that this may be because most marijuana users inhale more deeply than tobacco smokers and therefore hold the smoke in their lungs longer. The longer the smoke is in the lungs, the more the lungs are exposed to carcinogens. This suggests an increased possibility of developing malignant (cancerous) tumors in the respiratory system from marijuana smoke. Although marijuana smoke has been found to be a carcinogen, studies indicate that THC itself does not appear to be carcinogenic.

Would smoking more potent marijuana with a higher

THC content be less harmful, since users would probably smoke less to achieve the same high? Researchers asked this question and found that smoking more potent marijuana decreases its potential harm to the lungs only slightly. But more importantly, they found that the deleterious health effect of smoking any substance far outweighs the benefits of smoking "less" marijuana. Others have hypothesized that a marijuana user might inhale fewer particulates and tar when using a water pipe than when smoking a joint, but recent studies have disproved this theory.

Many experts take the position that all smoking-related diseases are dose-dependent. In other words, they suggest that what matters most when considering the health effects of marijuana smoking is the amount of smoke inhaled over time, not the amount inhaled per cigarette. Although they agree that marijuana smokers deposit harmful materials in their lungs, they cite studies that show that even heavy marijuana smokers (three to four marijuana cigarettes per day for about 15 years) never reach the smoke consumption levels of heavy tobacco smokers. In one study, over a six-year period, the health records of marijuana smokers were compared with those of nonsmokers of any substance. Researchers found that daily marijuana smokers were only slightly more likely than nonsmokers to visit their doctors for respiratory illnesses (36 percent compared with 33 percent). Studies also reported that most tobacco smokers over time show increased signs of pulmonary obstruction, an indicator of emphysema (a serious condition marked by loss of lung elasticity and shortness of breath). Heavy marijuana smokers did not show these same declines in lung function.

However, researchers on either side of the "dose-dependent" theory agree that marijuana smoke, like tobacco smoke, does contain cancer-causing substances. These researchers do not believe that one form of smoke is more or less dangerous than the other. They all agree that smokers who use both marijuana *and* tobacco have an increased risk of lung cancer because the total amount of smoke inhaled is greatly increased.

THE BRAIN

Research has not found definitive evidence of long-term permanent brain damage as a result of smoking marijuana. Some research has shown structural brain damage in rodents, but these studies used 100 times the amount of THC that would be a psychoactive dose for humans. In addition, these study results have not been duplicated in primate studies. A study of human marijuana subjects who smoked an average of nine marijuana cigarettes a day found no evidence of brain damage after assessing the brain with CT scans (computed axial tomography, also called CAT scans, in which film images are produced of cross-sections of specific tissue). However, many researchers point out that THC changes the ways in which the brain senses and processes information, most notably in the hippocampal region of the brain, and suggest that learning and memory behaviors are affected by marijuana use.

MARIJUANA, MENTAL ILLNESS, AND PSYCHOLOGICAL PROBLEMS

Many researchers have studied the relationship between marijuana and mental illness. Early twentieth century proponents of marijuana prohibition in the United States often cited studies showing a link between marijuana and insanity and referred to reports of large numbers of institutionalized mental patients in India and Egypt who had used marijuana. However, since the 1970s, researchers have effectively refuted the claims of a direct link between marijuana use and mental illness.

Although marijuana may not be linked to severe mental illness, research begun in the 1960s has suggested that marijuana can cause subtle psychological damage, particularly to adolescents. Studies have consistently shown that adolescents with psychological and behavioral problems are more likely than other adolescents to use marijuana heavily. Experts and others such as parents, school administrators, and drug abuse counselors often point to marijuana as the primary cause of these problems. They theorize that once marijuana is removed from a troubled adolescent's life, the troubles will soon depart as well. However, recent research discounts this theory. Most teens who use marijuana heavily are likely to have underlying psychological and behavioral problems. Therefore, heavy marijuana use may add to a teen's problems, but it is more a symptom than a cause of these problems.

CAN MARIJUANA CAUSE MENTAL ILLNESS?

A frequently cited study of 50,000 male Swedish military conscripts (draftees) supported the claim that marijuana causes mental illness. Originally, researchers observed a connection between the use of cannabis by age 18 and a diagnosis of schizophrenia later in life. It was suggested that men who had used marijuana 50 or more times by the age of 18 were more likely to be diagnosed as schizophrenic than those who had used marijuana less than 50 but more than 10 times. However, the interpretation of these results later proved to be flawed. All the men who received a diagnosis of schizophrenia had previously been given some sort of psychiatric diagnosis by the military at the time they were drafted. Each had at some point been in trouble at school or with the police, had come from broken homes, and had histories of psychological problems. Therefore, although heavy cannabis use may be associated with a variety of psychological and social problems, and even a later diagnosis of schizophrenia, it was a leap to suggest that the marijuana use had "caused" the schizophrenia. The claim of a "marijuana-schizophrenia connection" was further undermined when over the same period of time the number of treated cases of schizophrenia had declined while marijuana use had increased.

THE REPRODUCTIVE SYSTEM

Previous studies have claimed that THC delays sexual development in adolescents, interferes with male and female sex hormones, causes infertility, and produces feminine characteristics in males and masculine characteristics in females. Again, much of this research was conducted on animals using very high doses of THC; some of these conclusions were also drawn on the basis of very small-scale studies. Thus, many researchers feel that this uncertainty plus a lack of scientific data in humans suggest that there is no clear correlation between marijuana smoking and reproductive effects in humans.

Some studies in humans did find reproductive effects from marijuana; however, they were found to be temporary. For example, in a study in which men smoked up to 20 marijuana cigarettes a day (considered a very heavy dose), researchers found a decrease in their sperm concentrations. However, by the end of one month, sperm counts had returned to normal despite continued dosing of marijuana. This temporary effect was also shown in animal studies. In a study of female monkeys, high doses of THC resulted in hormonal changes and a disruption of their menstrual cycle. However, after six months of similar THC doses, the monkeys' hormonal levels and menstrual cycles returned to normal. Overall, the consensus of most researchers today is that THC has little impact on the reproductive system.

THE HEART

Eating or smoking marijuana has been shown to increase heart rate by 20 to 50 percent. This effect can occur within a few minutes to a quarter of an hour and can last for up to three hours. Because of the brain's tolerance to THC, it has been shown that these effects are temporary. However, marijuana users who do not know about or expect these acute health effects may find them unpleasant or even scary, resulting in panic or anxiety reactions. And, those with heart problems or other physical disorders may have disturbing or even harmful effects as a result of cannabis use.

4

Teenage Trends and Attitudes

Marijuana has the distinction of being the most widely used illicit drug by teenagers and adults in the United States. It has held this top-ranking position for at least 25 years. In fact, marijuana may rank only behind caffeine, alcohol, and nicotine as the most widely used drug in the world. Illicit drug use knows no geographic or economic boundaries and is considered one of the most disturbing social problems in the United States.

From the early to mid 1990s, teenage use of marijuana increased. This increase peaked around 1996 to 1997, and, since then, teen marijuana use has stabilized at these levels, showing little increase or decline.

HOW ARE TEENAGE TRENDS AND ATTITUDES MEASURED?

The U.S. Department of Health and Human Services (HHS) tracks the nation's substance abuse patterns through three major surveys: The National Household Survey on Drug Abuse (NHSDA), the Monitoring the Future (MTF) Survey, and the Drug Abuse Warning Network (DAWN). Statistical information from these surveys helps the United States identify potential drug abuse problem areas in order to set national drug policy and devote financial resources that target areas of greatest need. Data from these large-scale surveys are also used to develop prevention and treatment campaigns, with particular emphasis on programs aimed at youths aged 12 through 17. In 2001, the HHS devoted about 40 percent of its total yearly budget ($133 million out of a $3.3 billion total

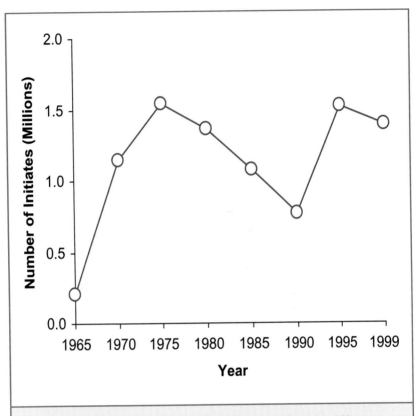

Surveys conducted by the U.S. Department of Health and Human Services track the U.S. population's drug use patterns. This graph from the National Household Survey on Drug Abuse shows the rate of teenage marijuana use over the last three decades.

budget) to youth-focused substance abuse programs.

The NHSDA is directed by the Substance Abuse and Mental Health Services Administration. Since 1971, it has provided annual estimates of the prevalence (patterns of use) of illicit drug, alcohol, and tobacco use in the United States, monitoring trends since that time. Results from this survey are based on a representative sample of the U.S. population 12 years and older. Marijuana-specific data are presented as a subcategory of "illicit drugs."

The MTF survey is funded by the National Institute on Drug Abuse. Since 1975, it has tracked illicit drug use trends and attitudes of 8th, 10th, and 12th grade students. These surveys ask students about lifetime use, past year use, past month use, and daily use of drugs, alcohol, cigarettes, and smokeless tobacco. Marijuana-specific data are broken out in the survey.

Despite differences in methodology, the NHSDA data and the MTF survey have shown similar long-term trends in the prevalence of substance abuse among youths. In addition to measuring prevalence, these surveys discuss teen perceptions of the harmfulness of drugs, their approval/disapproval of the use of drugs, and the availability of drugs.

For almost 30 years, DAWN has been an ongoing, national data system that collects information on drug-related visits to a sample of U.S. hospital emergency departments (ED). To be recorded, the ED visit has to be directly related to illegal drug use or to the nonmedical use of a drug. These data are used to provide information on some of the health consequences of drug abuse in the United States. DAWN does not measure the prevalence of drug use in the population, but does provide estimates of drug-related "episodes" and "mentions." An episode is the actual drug-related ED visit; the drug(s) thought to be responsible for the hospital visit are then "mentioned."

It is difficult to obtain marijuana-specific data from DAWN information, since up to four different substances can be recorded for each ED episode. And because a drug-related visit to an ED can have multiple drug mentions, not every reported substance may be, by itself, the cause of the medical emergency. Until DAWN data can provide more marijuana-specific information, many feel that policymakers cannot draw definitive conclusions about the consequences of marijuana use from these reports. DAWN researchers acknowledge this limitation of their data. DAWN, like NHSDA, is directed by the Substance Abuse and Mental Health Services Administration.

TRENDS IN MARIJUANA USE

When analyzing trends in adolescent use of marijuana, researchers usually discuss the *national average* trends. They do point out, however, that on narrower, individual levels, there are many subgroup differences based on gender, race/ethnicity, region of the country, college plans, socioeconomic level, and whether the teen lives in an urban or rural area. For this discussion, we rely on the national average trends; specific differences of these subgroups are reported elsewhere. It is also important to know when analyzing statistics that these surveys rely on self-reporting, a style that can contribute to some underreporting when teens are being asked to report illegal drug use.

The data from these three major surveys (NHSDA, MTF, and DAWN) provide a great deal of insight into recent trends in adolescent use of marijuana. Among 12- to 17-year-olds, the NHSDA reports:

- In 1999, the national average age of first-time marijuana use was 16.2 years old. Comparatively, the national average age of first-time alcohol use was 15.7 years old. (Other sources cite the average age of first marijuana use as 14, and first alcohol use at about age 12.)
- From 1990 to 1996, the number of first-time marijuana users increased significantly (from 1.4 million users in 1990 to 2.6 million in 1996). However, since 1996, the annual number of new users has fallen to about 2.0 million in 1999. These numbers show a steady decline in the number of teenagers who are trying marijuana for the first time.
- In 2000, 9.7 percent of adolescents reported past-month use of illicit drugs (meaning that an illicit drug was used at least once within 30 days of responding to the survey). Slightly over 7 percent of adolescents specifically reported marijuana use, with young men having a slightly higher rate of use than young women. Thus, past-month marijuana use constituted an overwhelming majority (73 percent) of adolescent illicit drug use.

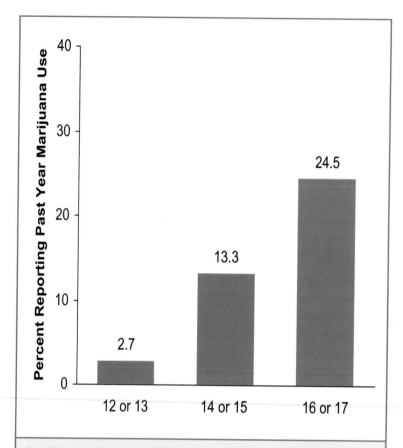

As this graph from the NHSDA survey indicates, teenagers are more likely to report past year marijuana use as they grow older, with over 24% of 15- to 16-year-olds reporting marijuana use in 2000. Peer influence and accessibility are determining factors in teen marijuana use.

Findings from the MTF survey on marijuana use among 10th and 12th graders add to this picture:

- After a period of significant increase in annual, monthly, and daily use of marijuana in the early 1990s, marijuana use peaked in 1997. Since 1997, its use among adolescents has held steady, with very few increases or declines from those peak rates. (Note: These figures

roughly correspond to the NHSDA data, which found
that the number of new users of marijuana peaked
in 1996.)
- Of high school seniors in 2001, almost half reported
having used marijuana or hashish at least once.

Over the past decade (between 1992 and 2001):
- *Past-month use* of marijuana increased from 12 to
22 percent among 12th graders and from 8 to 20 percent
among 10th graders.
- *Daily use* of marijuana increased from 2 to 6 percent
among 12th graders and from 1 to 4.5 percent among
10th graders.
- Comparatively, the *daily use* of cigarettes increased from
17 to 19 percent among 12th graders and has remained
constant at about 12 percent among 10th graders.

DAWN data follow similar trends:
- In 2000, patients aged 18 to 25 and 26 to 34 had the
highest rates of ED drug-related episodes, followed by
patients aged 12 to 17. Patients 35 years and over
accounted for the lowest rate of episodes.
- From 1999 to 2000, total drug-related ED episodes increased
20 percent for adolescents. Out of 63,448 mentions of
drugs, marijuana was mentioned 15,683 times.
- From 1994 to 2000, the rate of marijuana mentions
among 12- to 17-year-olds was virtually unchanged.
(Statistically, this rate showed very little change.)
- In 2000, 24 percent of all ED episodes involving marijuana
were "marijuana-only" mentions. Comparatively, nearly
half of all episodes involved "heroin-only" mentions.
(This is overall admissions, not specifically 12- to
17-year-olds.)
- In 2000, the majority (56 percent) of *all* drug-related ED
episodes involved more than one drug.

PREDICTIVE FACTORS: WHY DO SOME TEENS CHOOSE TO USE MARIJUANA?

Many researchers point to five factors that can predict the likelihood of marijuana use by teenagers: awareness, access, motivations for use, reassurance about safety, and a willingness to break social norms by violating the law.

Awareness

In the 1950s and early '60s, most young people did not know much about marijuana and other psychoactive drugs. In the mid- to late 1960s, this awareness exploded along with the Vietnam War and a sweeping movement toward "countercul-ture" activities. (Counterculture consists of values that are opposite to the norms of established society.) Thousands of young people "tuned in and turned on." Psychoactive drugs such as marijuana became a national expression of disaffection with what was seen as the conservatism of the 1950s and of a youthful quest for "freedom."

The media have also played an important role in creating awareness about marijuana, though not necessarily intention-ally. From news reports and "anti-drug" advertisements to dramatic storylines showing favorite actors smoking marijuana (whether advocating its use or taking an anti-drug stance), the media introduced marijuana to a mass audience.

Some researchers and policymakers feel it is important to continually maintain and pass on awareness of the potential dangers of marijuana from generation to generation. In this way, they feel teens can make informed choices about mari-juana use. This view is grounded in the theory of "generational forgetting"—the notion that it cannot be assumed that one generation will know the effects of using marijuana just because the previous generation knew them. These researchers attribute the increasing trend in marijuana use by teens to this generational forgetting theory, and they cite the millions of first-time adolescent marijuana users as evidence that each

J en and her best friend Alicia arrived late to the party. It was
10:30 P.M., and they saw that the evening looked promising.
Jen surveyed the darkened living room, hoping to see her friend
Kyle. No sign of him. Jen had a crush on Kyle, but he didn't
seem to notice that she wanted to be more than friends. The
girls saw that most of the kids were hanging out in the backyard.
As Alicia and Jen emerged through the screen door, Kyle yelled
"Hey!" and waved them over. He was sitting on the grass with a
group of their mutual friends, who scooted over to make room
for the newcomers. Kyle took a long hit from a joint, held his
breath, and passed it to Alicia, who had just settled down on
the grass. "Ya want some?" he asked through gritted teeth,
trying not to let the smoke escape his lungs. Alicia smiled, took
the joint, shook her head no, and passed it to Jen. Alicia knew
that Jen smoked pot, and she liked that Jen and her friends
were okay with the fact that she didn't smoke it.

Jen re-lit the joint, took a series of short puffs and then a
last long drag. She passed it to the girl on her right. A pipe soon
followed the joint, and in a few minutes Jen sighed with relaxation, lay back on the grass, and stared at the stars. Giggling,
she rolled over and poked Kyle. They began to talk animatedly
about a teacher's sense of fashion. From across the yard, Alicia
saw some girls dancing to a Grateful Dead song. She grabbed
a beer and got up to join them. About three hours later, Jen
dropped off Alicia and then drove herself home.

Jen and Alicia may not know that smoking marijuana can
diminish coordination and reaction times and could increase
the chances of having a car accident. Since Alicia had been
drinking, they should have made other arrangements with a
non-drinking, non-drug-using designated driver to get home.
They also may not know that marijuana smokers are at risk of
harming their lungs. And, of course, marijuana is illegal.

generation must learn anew about the potential hazards of using marijuana.

Accessibility

The availability of marijuana to teens has been tracked by both the NHSDA and the MTF survey. In 2001, MTF asked, "How difficult do you think it would be for you to get marijuana?" Findings include:

> The percentage of 10th graders who thought marijuana was "fairly easy" or "very easy" to obtain has increased over the past decade. In 1992, 65 percent of 10th graders had easy access to marijuana; this increased to 77 percent in 2001. Easy access to marijuana peaked at 80 percent in 1997 and has overall remained stable at or near those levels since then.

Interestingly, for 26 years (since MTF first began this survey), access to marijuana among 12th graders has been consistently high, averaging about 87 percent for over a quarter of a century.

Motivations to Use Marijuana

There are many reasons why teenagers enjoy getting high. Survey data over the years indicate that a majority of teens use marijuana to feel good, experiment, have a good time with friends, explore the inner self, and relax or relieve tension. According to these data, much of the motivation is celebratory in nature, and many teens use marijuana in social settings such as parties. Others use marijuana out of a sense of curiosity or adventure, the desire to "fit in" with a group of friends, or boredom. For every generation, defiance of parents can be a motivation to use marijuana.

Daily users often seem to use marijuana to deal with depression, anger, anxiety, and family/school problems and "to get away from problems." These negative reasons for getting

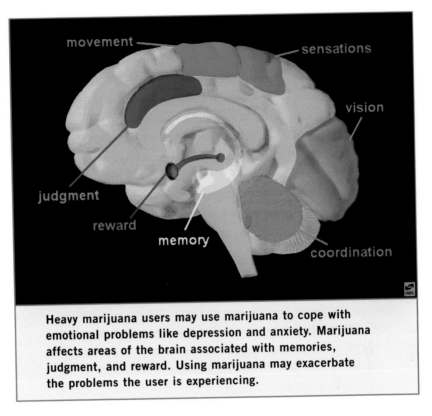

movement

sensations

vision

judgment

reward

memory

coordination

Heavy marijuana users may use marijuana to cope with emotional problems like depression and anxiety. Marijuana affects areas of the brain associated with memories, judgment, and reward. Using marijuana may exacerbate the problems the user is experiencing.

high suggest underlying psychological issues; as a result, daily users of marijuana may be more likely to become habitual, dependent users of the drug.

Reassurance about the Safety of Marijuana

Experts speak of "perceived risk" versus "perceived benefit" when attempting to understand the teenage trends of marijuana use. Most of our everyday decisions are based on a balanced scale of these two ideas. When deciding to do something, we weigh the pros and cons—the benefits and risks—and then make our decision. It is commonly believed that this risk/ benefit assessment is a primary factor in determining whether or not a teen will use marijuana.

In addition, studies show that information about the

perceived benefits of a drug usually spreads much faster along teen grapevines than does information about the potential risks of that drug. Evidence of a drug's risks usually takes longer to accumulate and become recognizable. Thus, misinformation about the risk/benefit ratio of marijuana use may be a significant contributor to its use. This view is supported by an analysis of NHSDA surveys from 1979 to 1996, which showed that adolescents ages 12 through 17 who perceived slight or no risk in occasional marijuana use were 12 times more likely to have used marijuana in the last year than teens who perceived great risk in using marijuana occasionally.

In further assessing the impact that the perceived risks of marijuana might have on teens, the 2001 MTF survey asked "How much do you think people risk harming themselves (physically or in other ways) if they try marijuana once or twice, smoke marijuana occasionally, or smoke marijuana regularly?" The data from this survey showed that fewer teenagers today perceive a risk from using marijuana in any of the manners described above than did their counterparts 10 years ago:

- Since 1992, the percentage of 12th graders who perceived "great risk" from trying marijuana once or twice declined from 25 to 15 percent.
- In 1992, 77 percent of 12th graders perceived regular smoking of marijuana as a great risk; in 2001, only 57 percent held that same view. Similar trends were reported among 10th graders.

Willingness to Break Social Norms and Violate the Law

Many experts observe that social norms about a drug are deeply influenced by the drug's legal status and whether or not it is considered dangerous. Since marijuana is illegal and considered by many to be harmful, its use is discouraged by most of today's American society. Yet, teenagers as a group often rebel against societal norms. Hence, it is not surprising that many teens use marijuana, or at least experiment with it, despite the consequences of clashing with parents, school authorities, and the law.

OTHER FACTORS THAT INFLUENCE THE DECISION TO USE MARIJUANA

Teenagers cite numerous motivations for their use of marijuana, and researchers have generated an equal number of hypotheses to explain what may lie behind its use. To better understand the teenage thought and decision-making processes regarding drug use, much discussion has focused on two important predictive factors: personality type and peer and parental influences.

Personality Type

A teen's basic personality structure is intimately intertwined with all other predictive factors of marijuana use. Researchers have long hypothesized that marijuana causes a teen to behave or act in certain ways. Often, heavy marijuana use in adolescence is associated with such traits as poor school performance, delinquency, acts of violence, laziness, mental health problems, and so on.

However, longitudinal studies on adolescents—studies that track the attitudes and behavior of the same group of students over a period of time—support a very different hypothesis. Such studies show that teens who use marijuana heavily tend to already have fundamental psychological and behavioral problems. For example, recent research shows that heavy marijuana users, when compared with their peers, performed poorly in high school *before* they started using the drug. Overall, although heavy marijuana use may add to a teen's problems, this latter viewpoint suggests that marijuana use may be more of a symptom than a cause of psychological and behavioral problems. Indeed, it is suggested that if marijuana is not available, a teen with these types of problems will simply find something else to take its place.

Many "personality theories" have been examined by researchers in relation to teen marijuana use. In one study, to categorize the personality differences between adolescent drug users and non-users, researchers created a scale of conventionality-unconventionality. In one study, the basic personality traits of young adolescents were categorized before their use of any drugs. Based on their personality traits, the adolescents were put into one of two groups: unconventional and conventional. Predictions were then made on who would use drugs (unconventional personality) and who would not (conventional personality).

Several years later, the (now) older adolescents were studied again. The predictive accuracy of the results was extremely high. The unconventional personality emerged as a key factor in drug experimentation and usage for older adolescents. In contrast to the conventional students, the unconventional students showed greater concern for personal independence, a lack of interest in the goals of institutions such as school or church, and a jaundiced (distasteful or hostile) view of the larger society around them. The study indicated that drug use and unconventionality were directly linked: the more unconventional the youth, the greater the likelihood of drug experimentation. In addition, this study indicated that the more unconventional the adolescent, the more likely he or she is to have a more serious drug involvement.

Peer Influence and the Disapproval Factor

Do teens urge other teens to use marijuana? Research points out that friends definitely influence other friends when it comes to using marijuana. However, this does not seem to take the form of coercion (defined here as "peer pressure") among teens regarding the decision to use or not use marijuana. In fact, research shows that marijuana use tends to flow from a more reciprocal relationship between friends. Thus, many researchers tend to speak about peer "influence" rather than "pressure" when describing this aspect of teen marijuana use.

Peer influence does appear to be one of the strongest factors affecting a teen's decision to use marijuana. Various studies and surveys consistently show that if teens have friends who use marijuana, they are more likely to use marijuana themselves. Those who do not have friends who use marijuana are less likely to use it themselves. Studies show that teens using marijuana tend to move toward new circles of friends who also use marijuana, simultaneously increasing peer acceptance, access to marijuana, and the influence of other marijuana-using friends. The more alienated a teen feels from friends and

IS MARIJUANA A GATEWAY TO HARDER DRUGS?

Many experts believe that marijuana use can lead to the use of harder drugs such as cocaine, heroin, and LSD. However, no conclusive evidence supports this direct cause-and-effect relationship. Studies in several countries, including the United States, indicate that most marijuana users never progress to other drugs. Teenagers who do go on to use other illegal drugs typically use tobacco, alcohol, and marijuana first. In fact, it has been shown that most teens use tobacco cigarettes and alcohol—before they are of legal age—before ever using marijuana. Also, many more teens use tobacco and alcohol than use marijuana. Thus, tobacco and alcohol may be "gateways" to marijuana use, although it is still not clear whether one drug can cause an individual to start using other drugs. Also, experts point out that psychological and behavioral problems, poor relationships with parents, or drug-taking peers who approve of drug use all are much more reliable predictors of a teen's progression to harder drugs than is the use of marijuana.

family, the more likely he or she is to progress to harder drugs such as heroin, cocaine, and LSD.

The 2001 MTF survey supports these findings. When asked, "Do you disapprove of people who try marijuana once or twice, smoke marijuana occasionally, or smoke marijuana regularly," here is what teens had to say:

- Across all three categories, within the past 10 years, reports from 12th graders showed a consistent decline in the number who disapproved of marijuana use.
- In 2001, about half of the 12th graders surveyed said they disapproved of people who try marijuana once or twice.
- About 63 percent disapproved of smoking marijuana occasionally, and about 80 percent said they disapproved of smoking the drug regularly. These percentages are substantially lower than those from the previous 10 years and highlight the evidence that the number of teens who disapprove of marijuana is decreasing.

It is interesting that there has been little change in the percentages of 10th graders who disapprove of marijuana use (across all three categories); yet their numbers are very similar to those of the 12th graders. For instance, in 2001, about half of the 10th graders disapproved of trying mari-juana; 66 percent disapproved of smoking it occasionally; and 78 percent disapproved of smoking it regularly. Indeed, over the past five years, these numbers have shown relatively no increase or decline. This indicates that the number of 10th graders who disapprove of smoking marijuana has remained stable.

Also, a recent NHSDA reports that:
- Teens with friends who "would not be very upset" if they tried marijuana are 16 times more likely to try marijuana than those whose friends would be "very upset."
- Teens with friends who use marijuana are 39 times more likely to use marijuana themselves.

Parental Influence

In a recent magazine advertisement by the Partnership for a Drug-Free America (sponsored by the Office of National Drug Control Policy), a teenage girl is pictured with the text, "Sure, I want my freedom, but without parental supervision, I'm much more likely to smoke pot and stuff. I hope my parents don't try to act like my friends. What I really need is parents." The text along the bottom of the ad reads, "Talk. Know. Ask. Parents. The Anti-Drug."

The content of this advertisement is based on research that shows that parents can influence a teen's decision-making process regarding marijuana use. However, it is possible that many parents who grew up in the 1960s and early 1970s (a time of widespread marijuana use) may feel hypocritical about speaking to their children about the consequences of using marijuana if they themselves used it. As a result, some researchers have argued that many of these parents neither create nor enforce guidelines or family boundaries surrounding the issue of marijuana use. Therefore, this advertisement (one of many in the national campaign against drug use and abuse) is aimed more at parents than at adolescents and invites parents to supervise and guide their teens rather than avoid the subject of marijuana use. In this way, the national ad campaign stresses the important role of parents in helping to deter their teenagers from using marijuana.

Results from the following studies support the strong influence of parents on the teenage use of marijuana. In a combined analysis (meta-analysis) of the 1979–1996 NHSDAs, researchers discovered the following trends in 12- to 17-year-olds:

- Teens whose parents ever used marijuana were about two to three times more likely to have ever used marijuana themselves. This parental influence did not vary among different racial/ethnic groups.

Results of surveys like the NHSDA indicate that parents have the power to influence their teenage child's decision to use marijuana or not. Parents who never used marijuana were likely to have children who never use marijuana. However, a teenager's perceived "lack of harm" related to marijuana use outweighed parental influence.

- Parental use of cigarettes or alcohol was more likely than parental use of marijuana to increase the risk of teen use of marijuana.
- Attitudes about perceived "lack of harm" from marijuana influenced teen use of marijuana more than parental influence. This association between marijuana use and a

perceived lack of harm from marijuana was five times stronger than the association between parental and teen use of marijuana.

- Parents who perceived little risk associated with marijuana had teens with similar attitudes. A recent NHSDA reports that teens are 9.6 times more likely to try marijuana if they have parents who "would not be very upset" if they tried it. Although some experts hypothesized that prior parental use of marijuana might influence teenagers, research has shown that baby-boomer parents (who grew up in a period of high marijuana use) did not account for the different rates of teenage marijuana use.

In addition, a 2001 survey by the Center on Addiction and Substance Abuse (CASA) revealed that "hands-on" parents who have established rules and expectations for their teens' behavior are more likely to have an "excellent" relationship with their adolescents than "hands-off" parents. Moreover, these involved parents are more likely to live with a teen at less risk of using drugs.

5

Marijuana Dependency

WHAT IS DRUG ADDICTION?

Drug addiction is a compulsive craving for a drug. It has several components. One component is tolerance—a need for ever-increasing quantities of a drug over time to maintain the same effects as when drug use first began. Since the body becomes tolerant to the effects of marijuana, users gradually feel less and less effect and therefore need to take greater amounts to achieve the same high. This phenomenon of tolerance can increase a person's dependence on drugs.

Withdrawal symptoms are also an important component of addiction. When a drug user stops taking a drug, he or she can experience a wide range of physical and/or psychological symptoms that will disappear if use of the drug is resumed. Some extreme users of marijuana suffer withdrawal symptoms, but these tend to be short-lived compared with withdrawal from harder drugs such as heroin.

Drug addiction is apparent when drug use is maintained despite significant physical and/or psychological cost to the user, and perhaps to family and friends. Some experts expand the idea of addiction to include abuse, which they define as the use of any drug, illegal or legal, in circumstances that threaten a person's health or impair his or her social functioning and productivity. For example, a student who cannot concentrate in school because he or she is stoned is "abusing" marijuana, just as cigarette smokers who have chronic bronchitis, yet continue to smoke, are abusing tobacco. Thus,

Researchers use equipment like this oscilloscope, which can measure levels of various neurotransmitters in the brain, in an attempt to understand the mechanisms of addiction better. While physical addiction does not appear to be a risk with marijuana use, psychological dependence on marijuana is a risk factor in its use.

addiction and, by extension, drug abuse can be summarized as a compelling desire to use a drug, a need for ever-increasing quantities of that drug, withdrawal symptoms if a drug is not used regularly, and continuation of drug use, regardless of circumstances or consequences.

DEPENDENCE ON MARIJUANA

Since all drugs have particular, self-defining characteristics, experts generally speak of a drug in terms of the user's dependence on it, rather than addiction. Although the two terms are very close in meaning, drug addiction is a special kind of dependence marked by physical changes in the body as a result of tolerance to and withdrawal from a drug.

Most research indicates that marijuana does not cause much physical dependence in most users. Therefore, such dependence tends not to be used as an indicator or predictor of marijuana use patterns. What research does show is that although marijuana usually does not cause physical dependence, it has the ability to create strong psychological dependence, as do almost all drugs. This dependence has many of the same characteristics of physical dependence—cravings, tolerance, withdrawal, and the continuation of the drug despite negative consequences. Psychological dependence therefore can be a useful tool for understanding marijuana use patterns.

Studies indicate that about 10 percent of people who try marijuana become dependent on it at some time during their four or five years of heaviest use. Trends show that marijuana use peaks during teenage years through about age 25; therefore, the "four or five years of heaviest use" likely correspond to some part of adolescence in most users. Other studies corroborate this finding, documenting that about 10 percent of young people using marijuana can be considered "problem users" (that is, people who use marijuana alone, and/or in the morning, and/or repeatedly). Problem users tend to experience other issues (such as dropping out of school or delinquency), but as we discussed previously, these behavioral problems have been shown to stem most often from other underlying problems rather than from marijuana itself. It is worth noting that the risk of becoming dependent on marijuana is similar to the risk of alcohol dependency (15 percent); nicotine dependency, by comparison, has a much higher risk (32 percent).

We can sense, intuitively and practically, how almost anything can create dependency. Some teens say they cannot live without chocolate. Others may just love to jog every day, rain or shine. Still others might read *Rolling Stone* magazine every month without fail or play poker for money every afternoon with their buddies. Researchers and teenagers alike often wonder, "How does psychological dependence differ from doing something repeatedly just because you like to do it?" Ongoing debate over the roots of addiction and dependency seeks to answer questions of this sort.

Many researchers suggest that the essence of dependence lies in the limiting of personal freedom. We are all dependent on food, water, and other people to live—no one is completely self-sufficient. However, what distinguishes drug dependency

ADDICTION: A STRANGE SORT OF MAGIC

"Addiction is a basic human problem whose roots go very deep. Most of us have at some point been wounded, no matter what kind of family we grew up in. We long for a sense of completeness and wholeness, and most often search for satisfaction outside of ourselves. Ironically, whatever satisfaction we gain from drugs, food, money and other 'sources' of pleasure really comes from inside of us. That is, we project our power onto external substances and activities, allowing them to make us feel better temporarily. This is a very strange sort of magic. We give away our power in exchange for a transient sense of wholeness, then suffer because the objects of our craving seem to control us. Addiction can be cured only when we consciously experience this process, reclaim our power, and recognize that our wounds must be healed from within."

[Andrew Weil, M.D., From Chocolate to Morphine, 1998]

from other "needs" is that it can take over and control a person's life, often at the expense of virtually everything else. Marijuana dependence can occur subtly over a period of time and can delude users into thinking they have not become dependent. Because the body becomes tolerant to marijuana's effects, heavy smokers can easily slide into an habitual routine of smoking more and more marijuana while receiving less and less of a "high." This adds to the possibility of becoming dependent on the drug without being aware of it. As each day becomes governed by how, when, and where drug use will occur, it is easy to see how marijuana dependency can limit personal freedom.

It requires a great deal of effort to break free from dependency on anything. Studies show that once a person becomes dependent on a drug, there is often no route to ending the dependency other than abstaining from drug use altogether. Unfortunately, many people who try to end drug dependency often wind up switching one dependency for another. Hence, we can see that dependency on drugs, including marijuana, can be a very serious problem with myriad negative consequences. It is therefore important that we examine in greater detail the physical and psychological aspects of dependence on marijuana.

Physical Dependence

Studies show that most marijuana users, even heavy users, can reduce or stop marijuana use with little or no physical withdrawal effects. Some extreme marijuana users do report physical withdrawal symptoms when they quit using the drug, including irritability, headaches, nervousness, and insomnia. However, these symptoms are temporary, diminishing within a few days to a few weeks, depending on the individual, and are usually portrayed as mild.

Studies show that marijuana does not produce the much harsher physical withdrawal symptoms experienced by heroin or alcohol addicts. Even heavy marijuana users can reduce or stop their use without physical withdrawal effects, since cessation of marijuana use typically results in rapid recovery from its effects (another aspect of the phenomenon of tolerance). Some researchers claim that heavy marijuana users who cut back on their use for even a short period can become sensitive again to lower doses of marijuana. (These researchers suggest that this can be a factor in avoiding dependence in the marijuana user.)

Many surveys indicate that a large majority of people who try marijuana do not become long-term frequent users. In a study of adults in their 30s who were first surveyed in high school, over 75 percent reported that they had not used marijuana over the past year. In another study, 85 percent of men who had been daily marijuana users from ages 18 to 28 were found to no longer be using the drug on a daily basis, although a majority continued to use it occasionally. These and other surveys and studies indicate that marijuana dependency is usually not as severe or long-term as it is for many other drugs. Still, everyone should be aware that marijuana dependency does exist; it is difficult to predict who will experience this problem and when it might occur.

There have been limited animal studies that show significant physical symptoms from marijuana withdrawal. For example, in a recent government-sponsored study, researchers gave mice large doses of THC continuously for four days, then administered a cannabinoid blocker drug, which immediately stripped THC from their receptors. This resulted in extreme physical withdrawal symptoms in the mice, suggesting that marijuana causes physical dependence. However, many experts in the field take issue with these findings, since when human marijuana users stop using marijuana, they always experience a *gradual* separation of THC from receptors (because of normal biological receptor functioning). These experts maintain that for this reason, humans do not experience severe physical withdrawal when they stop using marijuana.

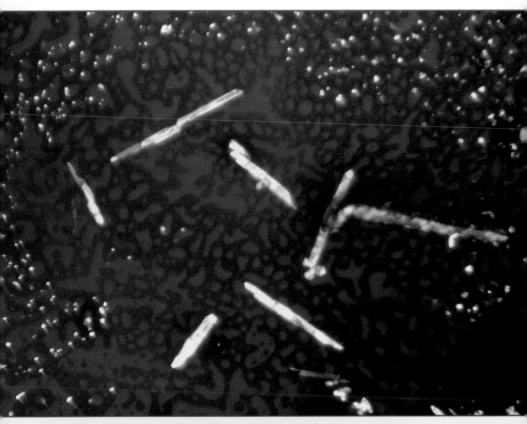

THC, shown here at 10X magnification, binds to CB1 and CB2 receptors throughout the brain and body. While researchers have produced physical withdrawal symptoms in laboratory animals by immediately stripping THC from these receptors, discontinuing marijuana use in real-life situations results in a gradual separation of THC from these receptors with no physical withdrawal symptoms.

Although there are fewer physical factors with marijuana dependency compared with many other drugs, breaking away can still be hard. As a result, heavy marijuana users who wish to reduce or stop their marijuana use often need to seek help from drug treatment providers or self-help groups. Research has found that most marijuana users enrolled in drug treatment programs are poly-drug abusers, who also report problems with alcohol, cocaine, amphetamines, tranquilizers, or heroin. Nevertheless, there has been a recent increase in the number of people entering drug treatment programs with a primary diagnosis of marijuana dependence.

Psychological Dependence

In looking at patterns of drug use and trying to predict its use, studies show that a person can be psychologically dependent on a drug without being physically dependent on it. For instance, after spending time in jail or in a treatment facility, many drug users often go back to using drugs, despite no longer having physical cravings or withdrawal symptoms. Research shows that physical dependence is "all or nothing"— the drug is either addicting or it is not—while psychological dependence operates on more of a continuum. Some drugs create more psychological dependence (such as cocaine), whereas others create a lesser dependence (such as marijuana). These findings help to explain how knowledge of psychological dependence can be a powerful tool in understanding dependence on drugs.

Still, it is difficult to generalize about the psyche of an individual teenager, and it is even more complicated to apply that characterization to thousands of other teens. Many researchers are attempting to decipher this teenage "code" with regard to drug-taking/decision-making processes. We have seen that actually a multitude of motivators and factors determine whether or not a teen will choose to use marijuana. Peer influence, personality type, access, conventionality, boredom, a desire to experiment, reduction of anxiety—these and many other factors strongly contribute to a teen's decision to use or not use marijuana.

Many study findings have hypothesized that marijuana causes psychological problems such as amotivational syndrome (lack of motivation), which links poor school performance to teen marijuana use. The assertion is that marijuana makes teens lazy and apathetic or that its use causes anxiety or aggression. However, the literature finds no conclusive causal links between marijuana use and a teen's behavior. Most experts believe the behavioral and psychological problems evident after using marijuana are typically created and have existed well before the onset of drug use.

TEENS AT RISK OF MARIJUANA DEPENDENCY

Because individual motivations to use drugs can vary greatly, it can be difficult to know which teens will experiment with marijuana and then stop and which teens will develop a dependency on marijuana. Although any adolescent can develop a marijuana dependency, some are at higher risk than others.

Some of those high-risk individuals may have one or more of the characteristics as follows:

- **Family conflict and discord**: Adolescents whose parents are often in conflict, frequently absent, or inconsistent in setting boundaries and guidance are more likely to use illegal drugs such as marijuana. Teens may use marijuana to cope with family stress, low self-esteem, depression, anger, and anxiety.

- **Detachment from peers**: Some adolescents, particularly girls who mature physically much sooner than others, may feel out of place.

- **Cognitive differences**: Adolescents with cognitive differences like attention deficit disorder or extraordinary intelligence may feel excluded from the mainstream, and find that drug use means ready acceptance among a group of new friends.

- **Drug-using friends**: Adolescents with friends who use marijuana are more likely to use marijuana themselves.

REINFORCEMENT: THE KEY MOTIVATOR

One of the keys to understanding psychological dependence on marijuana is the concept of "reinforcement." This is viewed by many experts as the underlying motivator of drug-taking behavior. Some researchers even believe that psychological dependence, based on reinforcement, is the driving force behind drug addiction. Reinforcement occurs when a teen receives a pleasurable sensation from using marijuana and is then motivated to use marijuana again to achieve the same pleasurable experience. The intensity of the pleasure that a drug delivers to the user is called a "reinforcer" of the experience. According to studies, taking a highly reinforcing or intensely pleasurable drug over a period of time leads to a powerful desire to repeat the experience (perhaps at the expense of personal or scholastic conduct). Thus, the more pleasurable the drug experience, the more reinforcing the user's experience and, therefore, the higher the drug's potential for psychological dependency.

Smoking marijuana is a very fast and direct way for THC to reach the bloodstream and the brain. The marijuana high can be felt in as little as 15 minutes. Because the pleasure felt by the marijuana user can be recreated easily and quickly, it is a very reinforceable experience.

Achieving pleasant or euphoric moods is clearly a perceived benefit of marijuana use. But it is equally important to recognize that avoiding unpleasant moods or situations can be another important motivator and therefore provides another dimension of reinforcement. Both experiences—pleasure or avoidance of pain or sadness—can lead the teen marijuana user to become psychologically dependent on marijuana. In fact, researchers believe that teens who use marijuana to seek relief from emotional pains such as anger, depression, and family/school problems experience even stronger reinforcement for repeated marijuana use than those motivated by a desire for euphoria. Since daily users often seem to use marijuana to deal with these negative psychological issues, they may be more likely to become habitual, dependent users of the drug.

We can see the ways in which reinforcement is a major contributor to marijuana dependency in teens. When a user has grown accustomed to having his or her feelings altered chemically, using marijuana becomes habitual; by this time, the teen user is likely to be displaying signs of psychological dependency on the drug. This use of marijuana in adolescence to avoid boredom, conflict, and other bad feelings is likely to establish unhealthy patterns of drug-taking, which can persist and cause problems later in life. Equally important, when a marijuana-dependent teen deals with most of his or her feelings by getting high, it often results in a failure to develop more skillful, effective ways of handling life's issues.

PREVENTING MARIJUANA USE: WHAT WORKS, WHAT DOESN'T

Many educators, researchers, policymakers, and social scientists believe that prevention of drug abuse is easier than and preferable to treatment for drug abuse. The earlier a possible drug dependency is identified in a marijuana user, the better the chance of correcting it. For example, researchers tell us that by understanding factors that predict teen marijuana use, young children can be identified as being "at risk" for use of drugs before they would use drugs. They suggest that informing potential young users about the effects and risks of marijuana use (or any drug), as well as exploring drug alternatives, may be an effective prevention tool.

Current U.S. anti-drug education and prevention campaigns increased in reach and frequency in the 1980s. Since then, adolescents have seen anti-drug messages practically everywhere: on shopping bags, comic books, restaurant place mats, billboards, television, bumper stickers, and candy wrappers. Beginning in elementary school, the DARE (Drug Abuse

Despite widespread anti-drug media campaigns, such as the Partnership for a Drug-Free America, marijuana and other drug use is on the rise. These campaigns strengthen anti-drug attitudes among non-drug users, but not among those teens already using drugs.

Resistance Education) program sends uniformed police officers into schools to teach about the dangers of drugs. As a result, today's teenagers have had more drug education than any group of young people in American history.

In spite of this drug education, past-month marijuana use among 10th and 12th graders has almost doubled in the last

10 years, and daily use of marijuana has increased even more. Thus, the efficacy of anti-drug education in America faces the challenge of a continuing trend of increased marijuana use among teenagers.

There is little scientific evidence to support the effectiveness of anti-drug messages or their impact on the drug-use decisions of adolescents. Media campaigns such as the Partnership for a Drug-Free America have yet to be proved effective in the reduction of illegal drug use among adolescents. Although these advertisements strengthen anti-drug attitudes among young children and non–drug-using adults, similar effects have not been seen in the attitudes or drug-using behavior of teenagers.

In a May 2002 news report, the head of U.S. drug control strategy and policy announced that the anti-drug advertising campaign aimed at American youth had failed to discourage teens from using marijuana and, in some cases, may have actually encouraged its use. The goal of this multimedia campaign, which began in 1997, was to reduce the number of young people who try marijuana. Analysis of data from the ad campaign shows that adolescents have been exposed to these anti-drug ads an average of 2.7 times per week. Several recent studies report similar findings about the DARE program and its impact on teenagers.

Over the last decade, past-month use of marijuana increased from 12 to 22 percent among 12th graders and from 8 to 20 percent among 10th graders. Daily use of marijuana increased from 2 to 6 percent among 12th graders and from 1 to 4.5 percent among 10th graders. Although there can be no debate that adolescent marijuana use has increased, one can look at these numbers from another point of view. In 2001, 78 percent of 12th graders *did not* use marijuana in the past month. Similarly, 94 percent of 12th graders *did not* use marijuana daily. Based on these and other findings, many researchers believe that most adolescent marijuana users are not regular users—but experimenters—of marijuana. This complex use pattern makes it all the more troublesome to decipher the effectiveness of anti-drug education or to determine what, if any, conclusive connections can be made between survey findings and educational programming.

ZERO TOLERANCE

The concept of zero tolerance drives much of today's legal and educational policy. The zero tolerance policies teach that using marijuana even once puts the user at risk for dependence and abuse of the drug. Most drug education programs are built around this zero tolerance message. Proponents of this policy stress that the purpose of drug education is to prevent drug experimentation; therefore, the topic of drug *use* is practically forbidden. In addition, as part of this zero tolerance policy, most schools impose harsh sanctions, including expulsion from school, for any use or possession of marijuana. Therefore, most students are reluctant to discuss their own drug use in drug education classrooms.

Also, most school-based drug education classes do not provide information about the relative risks of different drugs, doses, routes of exposure, and patterns of use. This presents a dilemma. Many educational and policy experts argue that the zero tolerance approach contradicts the natural propensity of teens to want to learn about and possibly experiment with psychoactive drugs (a propensity that is evident in the recent trends in marijuana use and attitudes among teens). Also, research has shown that prevention programs that use scientifically based information to teach adolescents about the relationship between marijuana use and its consequences play an important role in changing behavior. Thus, many experts observe that most drug education programs in American schools today do not provide much effective drug education.

In the 1970s, an alternative approach to drug education was endorsed by the National Institute on Drug Abuse. This

Former U.S. Drug Czar Barry McCaffrey attempted to find creative anti-drug school-based programs. Critics have questioned the effectiveness of approaches like zero tolerance, which prohibit a well-rounded drug education for students.

approach, devised by researchers, psychologists, and drug-policy analysts, declared that the goal of drug education was to reduce drug *abuse*, not *use*. They argued that moralizing about drugs was ineffective, that exaggerating the dangers from drugs was counterproductive (and might even lead more youth to try drugs), and that expecting adolescents to be totally abstinent was unrealistic.

Although this prevention approach was incorporated into some educational materials for a short time, it was abandoned in the early 1980s during President Ronald Reagan's campaign of "Just Say No" to drugs. Since then, zero tolerance has been the predominant educational anti-drug approach in American classrooms.

It is interesting that drug education in countries such as England, Australia, and the Netherlands often use a model known as "harm reduction." Proponents of harm reduction do not encourage or condone drug use, but they do assume that many adolescents will eventually experiment with psychoactive drugs. Since the goal is to reduce the harms associated with drug use, these programs actively educate adolescents about the relative risks of drugs and their responsible use. Most harm reduction education targets teenagers, since they are the age group most likely to begin experimenting with drugs. When comparing overall marijuana use in the United States (with a zero tolerance policy) with that in the Netherlands (with a more liberal harm reduction policy), recent statistics show that 34 percent of those in the United States over 15 years of age have used marijuana at least once compared with only 19 percent of those over 15 years of age in the Netherlands.

TREATING MARIJUANA DEPENDENCE

Most experts agree that treatment for marijuana dependence begins with the user's own recognition that he or she is dependent on marijuana and that this dependency is a problem in his or her life. Many successful self-help groups such as Narcotics Anonymous operate from a philosophy that effective drug treatment is entirely dependent on the individual's motivation to change. People who seek treatment assistance under duress or who are otherwise not motivated to take responsibility for their drug-taking choices are not likely to have successful treatment outcomes.

Most drug rehabilitation programs are designed to help manage the results of psychological dependence. These rehabilitation methods may include individual, group, and family counseling, often in conjunction with 12-step programs such as Narcotics Anonymous. These programs assist dependent drug users with identifying and understanding the motivators that drive their drug use. Since most treatment programs incorporate group therapy and since many teens may not relate well to adults, some experts believe that effective drug treatment programs for teens need to be geared exclusively to their age group. They suggest that being among other adolescents who share the same problem is likely to be therapeutic for teens who may feel isolated from peers.

How does a teen get referred to a drug rehabilitation program? A teen can "self-refer" on his or her own behalf or enter a program through intervention by a school, social service agency, temple or church, substance abuse or health care provider, or the criminal justice system. Data collected from TEDS (the Treatment Episode Data Set) indicate that the criminal justice system refers the greatest number of people to substance abuse treatment facilities. Justice system referrals, as defined by TEDS, include any referral from a police official, judge, prosecutor, probation officer, or other person affiliated with the judicial system. They also include court referrals for driving under the influence of drugs as well as referrals to treatment in place of prosecution of a drug offense.

TEDS correlates the referral sources to substance abuse treatment centers with the number of admissions to these facilities. Note that TEDS defines "admissions" as annual treatment episodes rather than the number of individuals entering treatment. Therefore, one person could enter treatment and be treated several times over the course of a year. These multiple episodes are counted as multiple admissions. When reviewing the findings below, keep in mind that the number of admissions is not the same as the number of individuals seeking treatment for drug dependency.

An analysis of TEDS data collected between 1993 and 1999 reveals the following:

- Marijuana was the most common drug of abuse among adolescent admissions (aged 12 to 17) in 1999.
- The number of adolescent marijuana *admissions* from all referral sources increased 260 percent between 1992 and 1999.

PERCENTAGES REPORTING PAST YEAR SUBSTANCE DEPENDENCE, BY AGE GROUPS: 2000

PAST YEAR DEPENDENCE	TOTAL	AGE GROUP (YEARS) 12–17	18–25	26 OR OLDER
Any Illicit Drug [1]	1.2	2.4	3.5	0.7
Marijuana and Hashish	0.8	1.8	2.5	0.3
Cocaine	0.2	0.2	0.5	0.2
Heroin	0.1	0.0	0.1	0.1
Hallucinogens	0.1	0.2	0.3	0.0
Inhalants	0.0	0.2	0.0	0.0
Nonmedical Use of Any Psychotherapeutic[2]	0.3	0.5	0.6	0.2
Pain Relievers	0.2	0.4	0.5	0.1
Tranquilizers	0.1	0.1	0.1	0.1
Stimulants	0.1	0.1	0.2	0.1
Sedatives	0.0	0.1	0.0	0.0
Alcohol	2.3	1.8	4.6	2.0
Alcohol or Any Illicit Drug[1]	3.2	3.5	7.2	2.4
Alcohol and Any Illicit Drug[1]	0.4	0.7	0.9	0.2

NOTE: Dependence is based on the definition found in the 4th ed. of the Diagnostic and Statistical Manual of Mental Disorders (DSM-IV) (APA, 1994).

1. Any Illicit Drug refers to marijuana/hashish, cocaine (including crack), heroin, hallucinogens (including LSD and PCP), inhalants, or any prescription-type psychotherapeutic used nonmedically.

2. Nonmedical use of any prescription-type pain reliever, tranquilizer, stimulant, or sedative; does not include over-the-counter drugs.

Source: SAMHSA, Office of Applied Studies, National Household Survey on Drug Abuse, 2000.

- The criminal justice system referred the majority (54 percent) of all teens to substance abuse treatment facilities in 1999.
- Criminal justice referrals of marijuana admissions for 15- to 17-year-olds increased 27 percent from 1996 to 1999.
- Adolescent marijuana admissions averaged 66 percent white, 21 percent African American, and 13 percent Hispanic between 1994 and 1999.

Many anti-drug policymakers suggest that the data that show a rising number of teen admissions to drug abuse treatment centers with "primary marijuana abuse" prove that marijuana creates high levels of dependency, especially among adolescents. However, according to *The DASIS Report* (a governmental report from the Drug and Alcohol Services Information System), the rising number of marijuana admissions is driven by an increase in treatment referrals through the criminal justice system. Indeed, *The DASIS Report* stresses that adolescent marijuana referrals to treatment through the criminal justice system increased at a higher rate than admissions through other referral sources. This raises the question of whether the increase in teenage marijuana admissions is the result of greater dependency on the drug or the result of stricter enforcement of marijuana laws. Thus, considerable controversy remains as to whether the increased number of teens admitted to treatment centers for marijuana abuse is a valid indicator of teen marijuana use or dependency.

RECOVERY

Once a frequent marijuana user clears the drug from the body and passes through any withdrawal symptoms, the journey to recovery begins. This is not an easy journey. It requires a complete reorganization and restructuring of thought processes, attitudes, and lifestyle. A marijuana-dependent teen may have organized nearly all daily thoughts and routines around obtaining or using marijuana. Recovery involves a conscious and deliberate effort to create new, more socially productive ways of spending time in order to focus on things other than marijuana. New focus can be directed toward work, hobbies, family, religion, and friends. In essence, experts suggest that recovering teens must change their entire social structure.

One of the hardest things for a teen to do is to stop associating with drug-taking friends. Peer influence is one of the strongest predictive factors of teen marijuana use. And so conversely, it is also the most effective deterrent to marijuana use. In other words, teens who do not approve of drugs are less likely to use drugs, either alone or with their friends.

Treatment programs of varying intensity are available, but all programs have the same fundamental mission—a marijuana-dependent person must maintain complete abstinence while learning to cope with the emotional and behavioral motivators associated with its abuse. Most of the feelings or motivations for using marijuana may still exist, but a great challenge for the recovering teen is to explore alternative ways of dealing with and expressing those intense feelings.

In many ways, this recovery process is similar to dealing with the loss of a loved one. Recovering teens may need to grieve for the loss of their past history as they move into a new, drug-free life. During such periods of bereavement, teens can experience feelings of depression and emptiness as families, friends, and familiar locations elicit memories of past drug use. Looking back, recovering teens can see how this bereavement period is a natural part of change and growth and is considered by many to be a healthy sign of a teen maturing to adulthood.

6

Marijuana and the Law

MARIJUANA'S LEGAL HISTORY

For most of American history, the cannabis plant has been used for medicinal and industrial purposes and was not well known for its psychoactive properties. However, in the twentieth century, marijuana began to be used more for its euphoric than for its medicinal effects. Although much mystery surrounds the debut of marijuana as a means of "getting high," it is generally assumed that smoking marijuana (in cigarette form) began in the early part of the twentieth century as groups of Mexican workers traveled across the border into the southwestern and southern states. Smoking marijuana also became a particular favorite of black jazz musicians in cities; thus, its use was associated almost exclusively with these and other minority groups.

In the 1920s, concerns about marijuana's psychological and behavioral effects increased, and a wide range of excessive behavior was associated with its use. Newspaper headlines reported a "marijuana menace," accompanied by stories linking marijuana users, notably immigrants and persons of color, to lurid crimes. Much of this "marijuana frenzy" later proved to be largely unsubstantiated. Today, researchers view marijuana's association with underclass and minority populations in the context of the racist fears and anti-foreigner prejudices that were prevalent at the time.

In 1930, the Federal Bureau of Narcotics was formed. By 1931, at least 29 states had prohibited use of marijuana for nonmedical

Law enforcement officials load truck after truck with marijuana plants after a police raid in California. The budget for the National Drug Control Strategy expands every year and funds programs that target both the supply and demand sides of drug use. As a Schedule I drug, marijuana is one of the prime targets of these programs.

(recreational) purposes. Studies on the properties and effects of marijuana were widely published, and the popular media sensationalized study results. Most of these studies were later shown to be inaccurate because of a lack of scientific understanding, and many medical, legal, and social policy experts termed the articles "propaganda" underwritten by the Federal Bureau of Narcotics.

Against a backdrop of mounting evidence of marijuana's harmful effects and fears about its moral and societal dangers, the federal Marihuana Tax Act was passed in 1937. This was the first federal regulation of the drug. Although the act was technically a revenue-producing tool, its actual intent was to prohibit the recreational (nonmedical) use of marijuana. According to the act, anyone who grew, imported, prescribed, or dispensed marijuana, including physicians and pharmacists, was required to register with federal tax authorities and pay an annual tax. Those who did not pay the required tax would be subject to criminal tax-evasion penalties. Thus, although the act did not make marijuana illegal, it did make its use expensive and inconvenient. By 1937, nearly every state had adopted legislation outlawing marijuana.

The 1950s marked the end of a phase of American drug policy regarding marijuana. The century had begun with limited concern about marijuana; by the 1950s, harsh penalties had been adopted on both the federal and state levels for its possession, use, or sale. By the end of the 1950s, many states had passed laws that made the possession of even small amounts of marijuana subject to the same penalties as for those who had committed violent crimes.

Despite legal efforts aimed at restriction, marijuana use continued to grow, with drug use during the second half of the 1960s and the early 1970s increasing sharply. The dramatic social upheavals of this period, including the Vietnam War and the "hippie" movement, all contributed to the growth and glorification of casual drug use (especially marijuana and hallucinogens). For the first time, marijuana use became mainstream, with millions of Americans from all walks of life, including young people, using the drug without apparent harm. Questions soon began to arise about the wisdom of the existing federal and state marijuana laws. Policymakers and government officials began to consider whether marijuana should be treated differently from other illegal drugs, particularly with regard to penalties for its use.

As a result, the 1970s ushered in a new era of marijuana legal policy that brought a general reduction in penalties for marijuana possession at both state and federal levels. The Comprehensive Drug Abuse Prevention and Control Act, passed by Congress in 1970, repealed all prior federal laws and reduced the possession or casual transfer of marijuana from a criminal felony (serious punishable offense) to a misdemeanor (lesser offense). Under this act, the maximum penalty for a first offense was a $5,000 fine and one year in prison. The act also allowed "conditional discharge" of first offenders, who could be placed on probation for up to one year and permitted their criminal record to be annulled after they satisfactorily completed a probationary period. These changes represented a trend toward the decriminalization of marijuana.

The Uniform Controlled Substance Act of 1970, drafted by the National Conference of Commissioners on Uniform State Laws, was designed to make state laws more compatible with the new federal law. Like the federal act, the Uniform Act recommended reducing penalties for marijuana possession

MARIJUANA AND PROHIBITION

Some experts theorize that pressure from the influential liquor lobby hastened legislation against marijuana in the late 1930s. The manufacture and sale of alcohol had been prohibited in 1919 by the adoption of the Eighteenth Amendment to the U.S. Constitution. The Twenty-first Amendment ended Prohibition in 1933, making alcohol legal once more. The 1937 Marihuana Tax Act and subsequent state laws making marijuana illegal were passed to the delight of liquor manufacturers, who saw the growing popularity of marijuana as a threat to their newly legalized profits.

from a felony to a misdemeanor. Over the years, many states have adopted the Uniform Act, but penalties still vary for marijuana possession. Some states made possession of marijuana for personal use a civil offense (misdemeanor) rather than a criminal offense (felony), with a traffic-ticket type of citation and a small fine substituting for arrest and jail time.

State penalties for second-offense possession and for selling marijuana vary widely. Sale is almost always a felony, with maximum sentences ranging from two years to life. Casual transfer is usually treated similarly to simple possession and does not tend to be treated as a felony. Most states treat the production/cultivation of marijuana as severely as they do sale of marijuana.

In 1972, the National Commission on Marihuana and Drug Abuse, formed by President Richard M. Nixon, presented its findings. After spending two years of comprehensive study on marijuana and the causes of drug abuse in general, the final report of the commission recommended a reduction in penalties for possession of small amounts (1 ounce or less) of marijuana for personal use. The commission also urged all states to adopt a uniform marijuana policy. Although the commission advised the decriminalization of marijuana, it resolutely rejected legalization. The commission maintained that social policy should continue to discourage the use of marijuana, but it emphasized that the "costs of a criminal prohibition against possession far exceeded its benefits in suppressing use." President Nixon rejected the findings of the commission, and instead opted to launch what became known as the "war on drugs."

Despite President Nixon's stance, in 1973, Oregon became the first state to decriminalize possession of small amounts of marijuana. Ten more states quickly followed, although specific legal definitions and penalties associated with decriminalization varied from state to state. In 1975, the Alaska Supreme Court ruled that the possession of marijuana for personal use by adults at home was protected by a constitutional right to privacy. This made Alaska the first state to have no legal penalties whatsoever for the possession of marijuana.

In 1977, President Jimmy Carter supported the decriminalization of marijuana, but this support waned over the course of his administration. In fact, the trend toward the liberalization of marijuana laws began to face growing resistance, especially from groups of parents who organized for greater focus on prevention. This position was bolstered by the release of findings from the National High School Senior Survey (begun in 1975 as part of the MTF survey), which showed an increase in daily marijuana use among high school students. Beginning in the 1980s, marijuana policy swung in the opposite direction from that of the early 1970s; the Reagan and Bush administrations resumed the "war on drugs," and by the early 1990s, possession of marijuana was a criminal offense in most states as well as under federal law.

In addition to this legal shift, an equally important shift took place in how the dangers of marijuana were viewed. In the 1930s, '40s, and '50s, national drug policy had focused on the acute effects of marijuana—for example, that a person might commit a crime while "high." By the 1990s, the chronic psychological, social, and related health effects of marijuana had become the focus of attention in policy.

MARIJUANA: A SCHEDULE I CONTROLLED SUBSTANCE

The mission of the Drug Enforcement Administration (DEA), a division of the federal government, is to enforce the drug laws of the United States. The DEA is a principal force in reducing the supply, and therefore the availability, of marijuana and other drugs. The DEA was established in 1973 under the U.S. Department of Justice and is responsible for enforcing the guidelines of the Controlled Substances Act of 1970. This act provides the legal foundation for today's national marijuana policy. It places drugs regulated under existing federal law, known as "controlled substances," into one of five schedules. Drugs are categorized by their distinguishing properties, including their potential for abuse and their medical usefulness; drugs within each schedule often produce similar effects. Schedule I is set aside for the most dangerous drugs that have no recognized medical use, whereas Schedule V classifies the least dangerous drugs as a group. In legal terms, any use of the substances controlled in Schedules I through V of the Controlled Substances Act is considered drug abuse and is subject to state and federal penalties.

Under the Controlled Substances Act, marijuana is categorized as a Schedule I drug (along with LSD and heroin). Schedule I drugs are defined as (1) drugs with a high potential for abuse, (2) drugs that have no currently accepted medical use in treatment in the United States, and (3) drugs that under medical supervision lack acceptable safety data. "Marijuana," as defined in Schedule I, refers to "all parts of the cannabis plant, its resin and its seeds, and any derivative mixture or preparation of the plant." It does not include the mature fibrous stalk of the plant (known as hemp), its derivatives, or sterilized cannabis seed that cannot germinate.

Schedule II drugs include Marinol (dronabinol), a synthetic version of THC in pill form, which has a currently accepted medical use in the United States primarily to alleviate nausea and stimulate appetite in cancer patients. Although Marinol may be legally prescribed and has been available for several

POSSESSION AND THE LAW

People found with illegal drugs on their person (or in their cars or houses) are considered guilty of possession. The consequences of a possession charge depend on the drug, the quantity of drug, and the state in which the person is arrested. In many states, merely being in the company of someone who is in possession of illegal drugs (even if you are unaware of the situation) can make you guilty of possession.

years to treat those and other medical conditions, many patients and physicians maintain that it does not relieve symptoms as effectively as does the smoking of marijuana.

For over 30 years, many groups and organizations have sought to lobby the DEA to move marijuana from a Schedule I to a Schedule II controlled-substance category. The argument is that marijuana is therapeutic for many serious illnesses and even more effective in some cases than conventional medicines. A Schedule II listing would permit physicians to prescribe marijuana and any of its components for patients whom they believe would have a medicinal benefit. In 1988 the DEA's own administrative law judge, Francis Young, said that significant "credible scientific support exists in favor of cannabis' medical usage." To date, however, the DEA has not moved marijuana from Schedule I to Schedule II.

CURRENT U.S. DRUG POLICY: SUPPLY AND DEMAND

Does the supply of marijuana drive demand for it, or vice versa? Marijuana-consuming countries such as the United States traditionally have blamed the suppliers of marijuana for its widespread availability. Drug-producing countries, on the other hand, counter that without foreign demand, local farmers would not be growing marijuana at all. It is obvious that teens could not use marijuana if they could not gain access to it; thus, reducing the supply of marijuana would reduce its availability. Others argue that preventing and treating marijuana use, and therefore reducing its demand, may be more important to the effective regulation of marijuana use.

When determining where to put monetary resources, U.S. drug policy aims to reduce both sides of the supply-and-demand equation. The 2004 budget for the National Drug Control Strategy, as requested by President George W. Bush, expanded budgets for programs that reduce demand for marijuana and other drugs. Demand-reduction programs for 2004 included new approaches to drug treatment and basic

Drug trafficking is big business: a police officer guards $35 million seized from drug kingpins in Bogotá, Columbia. The drug traffickers intended to use this money to buy cocaine for export to the United States.

research on drug use. The largest portion of the budget devoted to demand reduction was earmarked for educational and preventive programming directed toward children and adolescents. Budgets have also been increased for supply-reduction programs, such as law enforcement operations targeting U.S. sources of illegal drugs, enhanced patrols along trafficking routes to the United States, and an increase in security forces along U.S. borders (mainly in the Southwest). The 2004 National Drug Control Strategy budget was over $12 billion, with an increase proposed for 2005.

MARIJUANA AND THE JUVENILE JUSTICE SYSTEM

The first juvenile court in the United States was established in Illinois in 1899. The juvenile justice system was founded on the principles of rehabilitation, with a focus on the offender, not the offense. In the 1950s and 1960s, many began to question the ability of the juvenile court to effectively rehabilitate delinquent youth; by the 1980s, the pendulum began to swing away from lenient approaches and toward more severe sanctions for juvenile offenders. The 1990s completed this turnabout as authorities more strongly enforced the legal standards of juvenile crime.

Statistics show that juvenile arrest rates for drug abuse violations in recent years are substantially higher than those of a decade ago. This may suggest that juveniles have been breaking drug laws more often in recent years. However, it is equally possible that reduced tolerance for drug use has simply resulted in a greater willingness to arrest and prosecute juvenile

Mike knew Friday night was going to be special, and he didn't want to mess it up. He had been asking Mychelle out for two months. Now that she and that jerk she'd been dating had broken up, she finally told him yes. Mike's friend Bobby always got high and said he'd give Mike a couple of joints for his date with Mychelle as a "good luck" present. Thursday after school, Mike and Bobby drove to get a snack at the burger shop. Bobby handed Mike the two joints, and with a wink said, "Have a great time tomorrow night!"

Mike and Bobby may not know that, depending on which state they live in, even giving marijuana to someone (and accepting it) can be considered "dealing" drugs in spite of the fact that money may not be exchanged. Also, Mike and Bobby could pay stiff fines or even serve jail time for possessing, using, and/or selling marijuana. Getting arrested can interrupt or postpone a teen's hopes and dreams.

drug offenders. Therefore, a more careful analysis of these statistics is in order.

Several organizations collect data on juvenile arrests. The Federal Bureau of Investigation's Uniform Crime Reports (UCR) program, established in 1930, compiles crime information from nearly 17,000 state and local law enforcement agencies around the country. The UCR's main objective has been to produce criminal statistics for use in law enforcement. Today its "crime index" has become a leading public indicator of yearly fluctuations in the level of crime in the United States.

In 2000, the UCR estimated 1.6 million arrests for drug violations in the United States among all age groups. The UCR defines drug violations as "state and/or local offenses related to the unlawful sale, purchase, distribution, manufacture, cultivation, possession, or use of a narcotic drug." These reports consider marijuana a narcotic drug.

When interpreting UCR data, we can assume that a juvenile is someone who is under 18 years of age. We should also note that recent UCR data are not specific to juvenile *marijuana* arrest trends; its findings relate to *overall* juvenile drug abuse arrest trends, regardless of the type of drug involved.

According to recent Uniform Crime Reports data:

- Between 1991 and 2000, across all age groups, drug abuse arrests increased by about 50 percent.
- By comparison, juvenile drug arrests increased 145 percent in that same 10-year period. (In 1991, about 43,000 juveniles were arrested for drug abuse violations; in 2000, 106,000 juveniles were arrested on the same charges.)
- However, much of this increase occurred between 1991 and 1995; between 1996 and 2000, juvenile arrests stabilized, averaging a 5 percent fluctuation. Drug arrests between 1996 and 2000 decreased for juvenile males by 5 percent and increased for females by 5 percent.
- It is worth noting that in 2000, approximately 94,000 juvenile males were arrested on drug abuse charges

compared with 17,000 females in that same year. Historically, there have typically been more arrests of juvenile males than females for drug abuse violations.

- In 1997, about 1.5 million pounds of marijuana were seized by the federal government. In 2000, the amount of confiscated marijuana nearly doubled to 2.6 million pounds.
- In 2000, 81 percent of drug abuse arrests for all age groups were for drug possession. Marijuana arrests accounted for 41 percent of all possession arrests compared with 24 percent for heroin or cocaine arrests. Of those arrested for possession of marijuana, over half were from the midwestern and southern regions of the United States.
- In addition, 11 percent of juveniles living in rural areas were arrested for drug violations in 2000 compared with only 7 percent of those living in cities.

THE GREAT DEBATE: LEGALIZING MEDICAL MARIJUANA

The decriminalization and legalization of marijuana are intricately woven into the medical marijuana movement. Essentially, it is a debate over the value of marijuana's medicinal properties compared with the risks posed by its use. NORML, the National Organization for the Reform of Marijuana Laws, has been in the forefront of this 30-year controversy since they first petitioned in 1972 to move marijuana to a Schedule II category. NORML and other proponents of medical marijuana maintain that when compared with drugs such as heroin and cocaine, marijuana is not only safe but holds great potential as a prescription drug.

If marijuana were moved to Schedule II, physicians would be able to legally prescribe marijuana without fear of losing their medical licenses. As a Schedule II drug, marijuana would be prescribed under the same strict regulations that govern the medical prescription of morphine and cocaine. In 1989,

NORML petitioned the DEA to reclassify marijuana, but was again denied. Today, marijuana remains a Schedule I controlled substance. Despite the threat of arrest for using an illegal drug, many people who suffer debilitating illnesses use marijuana medicinally today.

As part of its support for the legalization of medical marijuana, NORML advocates the *complete* decriminalization of marijuana, a step that would remove *all* penalties for the private possession and the responsible use of marijuana by adults. Under this scenario, private marijuana users, including those with serious medical conditions, would not be arrested, but large-scale commercial sellers would still be violating drug laws. NORML also calls for the development of a legally controlled market for marijuana in which adult consumers could buy marijuana for personal use from safe, legal sources.

Opponents of the medical marijuana movement claim that NORML (and others who support NORML's view) merely justifies its own "pro-marijuana" agenda by endorsing marijuana's medical benefits. They assert that marijuana supporters are exploiting public sympathy for seriously ill patients as a way of advancing their own platform of complete legalization of marijuana. These opponents express concern that the legalization of medical marijuana could lead teens to underestimate the risks associated with the drug. They are also concerned that such action would increase overall marijuana use and dependency and perhaps even result in the decriminalization of more harmful drugs.

Many prominent people and organizations have supported the legalization of medical marijuana, including the American Public Health Association, former U.S. Surgeon General Joycelyn Elders, national associations of prosecutors and criminal defense attorneys, and the editorial boards of numerous newspapers, among others. Public opinion polls conducted by TIME/CNN in October 2002 report that approximately 80 percent of the American public supports patient access

Many terminally ill patients find relief from pain and nausea by using marijuana. Proponents of marijuana's legalization or reclassification as a Schedule II drug, like this protester in Florida, believe its benefits as a potential medicine outweigh its risks.

to marijuana. In addition, many experts feel that no convincing data support the concerns of those opposed to medical marijuana, especially if the medical use of the drug is regulated as closely as other legal medications with abuse potential. Opponents hold firm, citing the health and behavioral risks from smoking marijuana and claiming that medical marijuana is a social and emotional, not a medical, issue.

Although using marijuana for medical purposes is illegal because U.S. federal law classifies marijuana as a Schedule I drug, states are not obligated to mirror federal laws. Many states have therefore created their own provisions for the medicinal use of marijuana. For example, in the 1970s,

35 states passed laws supporting marijuana's use as a medicine. In 1996, voters in California and Arizona passed two referendums (Proposition 215 in California and Proposition 200 in Arizona) supporting legalization of the medical use of marijuana under certain conditions. The Clinton administration opposed both these efforts, threatening to criminally prosecute physicians or revoke their licenses to prescribe controlled substances if they recommended smoking marijuana to their patients.

Since some state marijuana laws are at odds with federal laws, their implementation raises complex legal questions. For example, federal law prevents states from making marijuana supplies legally available. Therefore, although it is legal in some states to use marijuana for medical purposes, it is not possible to obtain the drug legally because of federal law.

A recent 2002 U.S. Supreme Court decision upheld the federal government's position on the illegality of marijuana by shutting down "cannabis buyers' clubs" that supplied marijuana to medically needy patients. These clubs were established under California's Proposition 215 to supply marijuana to more than 8,000 patients. The Supreme Court found that the federal Controlled Substances Act contained "no exception that would allow patients to use the drug after exhausting all other remedies." Although the passage of related state laws removed the threat of state prosecution for patients who use the drug, the threat of federal prosecution continues to exist, notably for physicians and their medical licenses.

Today, eight states in addition to California have legalized marijuana for medical purposes. Some allow patients to grow a limited number of marijuana plants for personal use without fear of state prosecution. Believing that the federal government ruled against the California buyers' clubs because large amounts of marijuana were being grown in a central location and distributed to large numbers of patients, the states that have authorized the cultivation of small amounts of marijuana hope in this way to avoid governmental opposition.

The marijuana-legalization debate became the primary focus of the midterm elections in Nevada on November 5, 2002. A group known as Nevadans for Responsible Law Enforcement proposed a marijuana-legalization initiative that appeared as Question 9 on Nevada's 2002 general election ballot. If the initiative had passed in this election and then again in November 2004, it would have amended the state's constitution to allow anyone 21 years old or older to use or possess up to three ounces of marijuana without legal or criminal ramifications. While only 39 percent of Nevada's voters supported the initiative, this percentage seems to mirror the growing national trend of support for marijuana legalization: According to a TIME/CNN poll conducted in October 2002, 34 percent of Americans think marijuana should be legalized— a percentage that has almost doubled since 1986.

The controversy surrounding the use of marijuana is all-encompassing. Its reach knows no boundary, affecting adolescents and adults in every geographic pocket of the United States and throughout the world. Expert opinions remain sharply divided over the health and behavioral risks of using marijuana, over appropriate social policy, over its role in medicine, and over its legal ramifications. Who knows what the future has in store for marijuana? All we can say for certain is that marijuana's future remains an important and fascinating topic.

Bibliography

Albert, Tanya. Nevada approves bill on medical use of marijuana. *American Medical News* 44 (2001): 13.

Belenko, Steven R. *Drugs and Drug Policy in America.* Westport, Conn.: Greenwood Press, 2000.

Drug and Alcohol Services Information System (DASIS). *The DASIS Report: Treatment Referral Sources for Adolescent Marijuana Users.* Substance Abuse and Mental Health Services Administration, Office of Applied Studies, 2002.

Drug Enforcement Administration. *Drug Classes.* Obtained May 2002 from *http://www.usdoj.gov/dea.*

Federal Bureau of Investigation. *Crime in the United States 2000: Uniform Crime Reports.* Washington, D.C.: U.S. Department of Justice, 2000.

Geiwitz, James. *THC in Hemp Foods and Cosmetics: The Appropriate Risk Assessment.* Obtained May 2002 from Canadian Ad Hoc Committee on Hemp Risks, www.industrrialhemp.net.

Goldberg, Raymond. *Taking Sides. Clashing Views on Controversial Issues in Drugs and Society,* 3rd ed. Guilford, Conn.: Dushkin/McGraw-Hill, 1998.

Goode, Erich. *Drugs in American Society,* 4th ed. New York: McGraw-Hill, 1993.

Grinspoon, Lester and James B. Bakalar. *Marijuana, The Forbidden Medicine.* New Haven, Conn.: Yale University, 1993.

Grinspoon, Lester. *Marihuana Reconsidered.* Oakland, Ca.: Quick American Archives, 1994.

Hall, Wayne, and Nadia Solowij. Adverse effects of cannabis. *The Lancet* 352: 1611-1616, 1998.

Iversen, Leslie L. *The Science of Marijuana.* New York: Oxford University Press, 2000.

Jaffe, Jerome H. *Encyclopedia of Drugs and Alcohol* (Volume 2). New York: Simon & Schuster Macmillan, 1995.

Johnston, L.D., P.M. O'Malley, and J.G. Bachman. *Monitoring the Future National Results on Adolescent Drug Use: Overview of Key Findings, 2001.* National Institute on Drug Abuse (NIH Publication No. 02-5105), 2002.

Johnston, L.D. *Reasons for Use, Abstention, and Quitting Illicit Drug Use by American Adolescents.* Monitoring the Future Occasional Paper #44. Ann Arbor, Mich.: University of Michigan Press, 1998.

Joy, Janet E., Stanley J. Watson, Jr., and John A. Benson, Jr. *Marijuana and Medicine: Assessing the Science Base.* Institute of Medicine. Washington, D.C.: National Academy Press, 1999.

Kandel, Denise, and Pamela Griesler, et al. *Parental Influences on Adolescent Marijuana Use and the Baby Boom Generation: Findings from the 1979-1996 NHSDA.* Substance Abuse and Mental Health Services Administration, Office of Applied Studies, 2001.

Landers, Susan J. Supreme Court ruling undermines medical use of marijuana. *American Medical News* 44 (2001): 29.

National Center on Addiction and Substance Abuse (CASA). *The National Survey of American Attitudes on Substance Abuse VI: Teens.* 2001. *http://www.casacolumbia.org.*

National Drug Control Strategy: FY 2003 Budget Summary. Washington, D.C.: The White House, 2002.

National Institute on Drug Abuse. *National Conference on Marijuana Use: Prevention, Treatment, and Research.* NIH Publication No. 96-4106, 1996.

National Organization for the Reform of Marijuana Laws (NORML). *Statement on the Cultivation of Industrial Hemp,* 2002. *http://www.norml.org.*

National Organization for the Reform of Marijuana Laws (NORML). *NORML's Testimony on Marijuana Decriminalization Before Congress (1999) Keith Stroup, Esq,* 1999. *http://www.norml.org.*

National Organization for the Reform of Marijuana Laws (NORML). *Unintended Consequences! Drug Czar Admits Federal Anti-Drug Ads Having Opposite Effect on Teens,* 2002. *http://www.norml.org.*

National Research Council of the National Academy of Sciences. *An Analysis of Marijuana Policy.* Schaffer Library of Drug Policy, 1982. *http://www.druglibrary.org.*

The *New Encyclopaedia Britannica,* vol. 5, 15th ed. *Marijuana.* 2002.

The *New Encyclopaedia Britannica,* vol. 13, 15th ed. *Alcohol and Drug Consumption.* 2002.

Nolin, Pierre Claude and Colin Kenny. *Discussion Paper on Cannabis.* Ontario, Canada: The Senate Special Committee on Illegal Drugs, 2002.

North American Industrial Hemp Council. *Hemp Facts Sheet* 1997. *http://www.naihc.org.*

Office of National Drug Control Policy. Partnership for a Drug-Free America advertisement. *National Geographic* (Spring) 2002.

Ottomanelli, Gennaro. *Children and Addiction.* Westport, Conn.: Praeger Publishers, 1995.

Perfetto, Sarah. Industrial hemp can save the world. *Napa Valley Register.* Pulitzer Newspapers, Inc., 2002.

Roza, Greg. *The Encyclopedia of Drugs and Alcohol.* Baltimore: The Rosen Publishing Group, 2001.

Snyder, Howard N. and Melissa Sickmund. *Juvenile Offenders and Victims: 1999 National Report.* Washington, D.C.: Office of Juvenile Justice and Delinquency Prevention, 1999.

Snyder, Solomon H. *Drugs and the Brain.* Philadelphia: Chelsea House Publishers, 1987.

Stein, Joel. "Is America Going to Pot?" *TIME Magazine,* November 2002, 56–62.

Substance Abuse and Mental Health Services Administration. *Summary of Findings from the 2000 National Household Survey on Drug Abuse.* NHSDA Series: H-13, DHHS Publication No. SMA 01-3549, 2001.

Substance Abuse and Mental Health Services Administration, Office of Applied Studies. *Emergency Department Trends from the Drug Abuse Warning Network, Preliminary Estimates January-June 2001 with Revised Estimates 1994 to 2000.* DAWN Series D-20, DHHS Publication No. (SMA) 02-3634, 2002.

Weil, Andrew and Winifred Rosen. *From Chocolate to Morphine.* Boston: Houghton Mifflin Company, 1998.

Zimmer, L. and J.P. Morgan. *Marijuana Myths, Marijuana Facts: A Review of the Scientific Evidence.* New York: The Lindesmith Center, 1997.

Further Reading

Alternatives to Drugs

Cousins, Norman. *Anatomy of an Illness.* Boston: G.K. Hall, 1980.

Weil, Andrew. *The Marriage of the Sun and Moon: A Quest for Unity in Consciousness.* Boston: Houghton Mifflin, 1980.

Critical Thinking

Bakalar, James B. and Lester Grinspoon. *Drug Control in a Free Society.* Cambridge, Mass.: Cambridge University Press, 1984.

Goldberg, Raymond. *Taking Sides. Clashing Views on Controversial Issues in Drugs and Society,* 3rd ed. Guilford, Conn.: Dushkin/McGraw-Hill, 1998.

Dependency

Wilshire, Bruce. *Wild Hunger.* Lanham, Md.: Rowman & Littlefield Publishers, 1999.

General

Abel, Ernest L. *Marihuana: The First Twelve Thousand Years.* New York: Plenum Press, 1980.

Iversen, Leslie L. *The Science of Marijuana.* New York: Oxford University Press, 2000.

Marijuana and Medicine

Joy, Janet E., Stanley J. Watson, Jr., and John A. Benson, Jr. *Marijuana and Medicine: Assessing the Science Base.* Washington, D.C.: Institute of Medicine, National Academy Press, 1999.

Mack, Alison and Janet Joy. *Marijuana as Medicine?* Washington, D.C.: Institute of Medicine, National Academy Press, 2001.

Index

Picture Credits

About the Author

Randi Mehling holds a Bachelor's in Journalism and a Master of Public Health from Rutgers University. Throughout her career, she has combined her passion for writing with her interest in healthcare and the environment. In addition to writing nonfiction for young adults, Randi has published in academic journals such as *Trends in Health Care, Law & Ethics*, designed educational programs for chronically ill patients, is a published poet, and is currently working on her first novel. Her commitment to education has led her to teach martial arts to children and Spanish to adults. She and her husband Rod live in the New Jersey countryside and dedicate this book to Sasha.

About the Editor

David J. Triggle is a University Professor and a Distinguished Professor in the School of Pharmacy and Pharmaceutical Sciences at the State University of New York at Buffalo. He studied in the United Kingdom and earned his B.Sc. degree in Chemistry from the University of Southampton and a Ph.D. degree in Chemistry at the University of Hull. Following post-doctoral work at the University of Ottawa in Canada and the University of London in the United Kingdom, he assumed a position at the School of Pharmacy at Buffalo. He served as Chairman of the Department of Biochemical Pharmacology from 1971 to 1985 and as Dean of the School of Pharmacy from 1985 to 1995. From 1995 to 2001 he served as the Dean of the Graduate School, and as the University Provost from 2000 to 2001. He is the author of several books dealing with the chemical pharmacology of the autonomic nervous system and drug-receptor interactions, some four hundred scientific publications, and has delivered over one thousand lectures worldwide on his research.